A Trail

of the

Holy Spirit

The Light within—a Missionary
Call to the Wild

GAIL GORDON

ISBN 979-8-88751-132-0 (paperback)
ISBN 979-8-88751-133-7 (digital)

Copyright © 2023 by Gail Gordon

All rights reserved. No part of this publication may be reproduced, distributed, or transmitted in any form or by any means, including photocopying, recording, or other electronic or mechanical methods without the prior written permission of the publisher. For permission requests, solicit the publisher via the address below.

Christian Faith Publishing
832 Park Avenue
Meadville, PA 16335
www.christianfaithpublishing.com

Printed in the United States of America

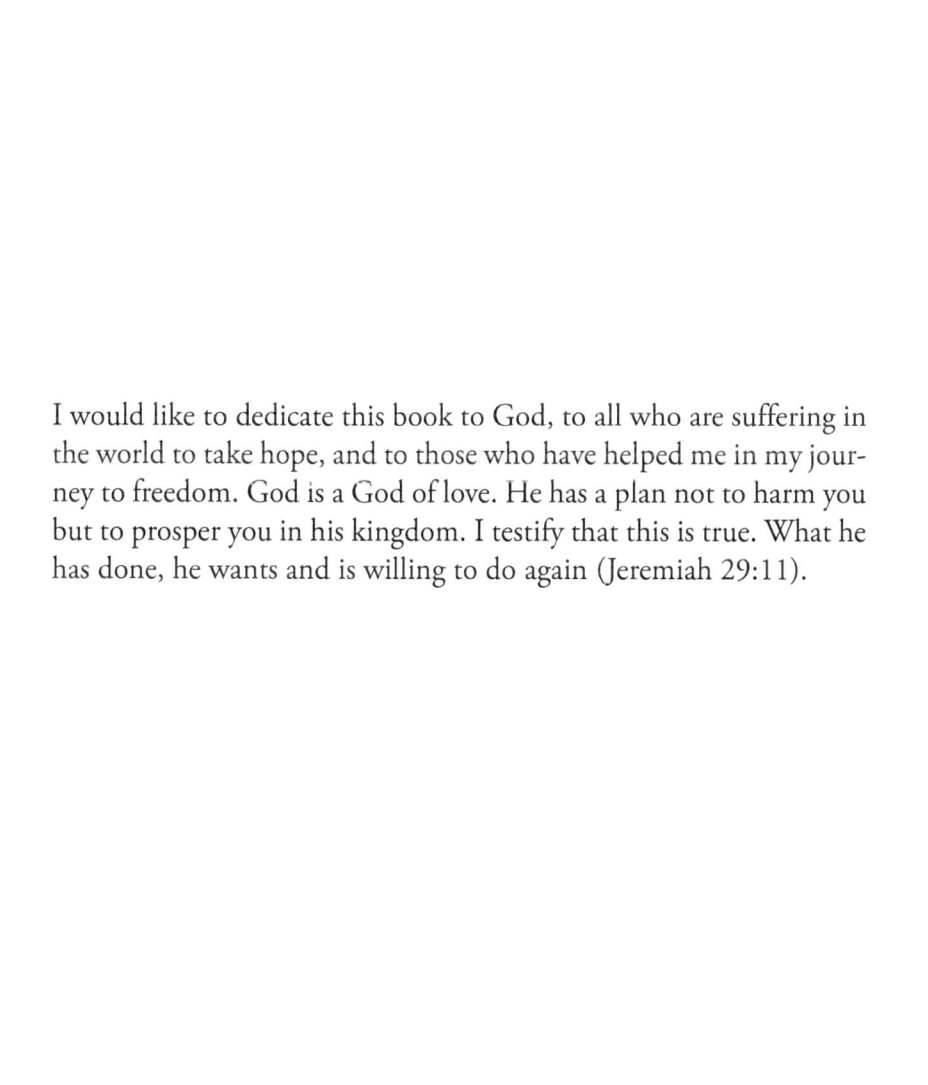

I would like to dedicate this book to God, to all who are suffering in the world to take hope, and to those who have helped me in my journey to freedom. God is a God of love. He has a plan not to harm you but to prosper you in his kingdom. I testify that this is true. What he has done, he wants and is willing to do again (Jeremiah 29:11).

Contents

Acknowledgments vii
Endorsements ix
Foreword xiii
Introduction xvii
1: The Hidden Crown 1
2: The American 14
3: Nine Women in the Jungle 31
4: The House by the Water 51
5: The Mission 66
6: The Children 77
7: The Missionaries 91
8: Victory, Defiance, and Darkness 115
9: Don't Fight the River 125
10: The Journey Isn't Over 136

Acknowledgments

Evelyn Cunningham, my mom, who prayed and instilled the love of God into my heart.

Frank Cunningham, my father, for establishing strength in my spirit. When I fell off the horse, I always had to get back on to have the victory.

Ted Gordon, my husband, who has stood by me through thick and thin. You are the best.

Trevor Gordon, my son. No one compares to you.

Richard Stanczyk for believing in me when I did not believe in myself.

Christi Dupre, you are my Aaron holding up my arms when my own strength fails. God bless you.

Carolyn Jimenez and our small group for always speaking truth and keeping our focus as we stepped out of the box into greater faith.

Allen Sappington, thank you for being my greatest cheerleader. Your love and joy expressed has built my confidence. You have a special place in my heart.

Racheal Timmerman Dilka, I love walking side by side with you to bring life to the nations!

Sylvia Rivas Maltzman, I thank God for your brilliance, guidance, and love given to *A Trail of the Holy Spirit*.

Pastor Marlin, thank you for opening the Bible to Deuteronomy 18:9–13. Your confidence in the Lord is contagious.

My friends, family, church, and those who have crossed my path in life, depositing the unique gift of themselves.

Endorsements

"Why am I here?" It is a question that Gail asks herself over and over again in this book and one each of us attempts to answer. "Have you ever stopped, taken a look at your life, and wondered how you got there?" Gail does this and shares her life story of discovering the person of the Holy Spirit. Through many dreams, encounters, and experiences, Gail concludes that answering the call of God is the "greatest life one can lead, and where it will go has endless possibilities." As she recounts many twists, turns, and even terrifying moments all over the world, Gail shows why full—deep—surrender leads to an adventure with God. Each chapter in her story illustrates the importance of trading the bonds of fear with the freedom of faith. Just jump in and "don't fight the river" as you discover that life in the Spirit is more about the process than the destination!

—Doreen Morehouse
Instructor, Global Awakening's College of Ministry

Reading *A Trail of the Holy Spirit* was enjoyable, encouraging, and enlightening. I obviously was in the middle of and experiencing many of the events and things written about in this book. What is special about reading this book is Gail's ability to recognize the many ways the Holy Spirit is working in our lives and pursuits as we pursue his will. If I'm honest, there are many parts of the book that I was experiencing with Gail that I was just taking at face value. Gail brings to life with words how active the Holy Spirit is in almost all we do especially when we are carrying out what we believe is his will for us.

It is evident that God uses dreams and visions as a way to communicate with us. It is always upon us to test the spirit and be sure it aligns with God's Word.

I want to thank Gail for having the courage, work ethic, willingness, and faithfulness to carry out the work of Casa Agua Azul.

God can use anyone to do anything. Gail did not let feelings of inadequacy or possibly not having the tools to accomplish this dream stop her. God will surround you with who you need and resources to accomplish his will. Thanks be to God and all the beautiful supporters of Casa Agua Azul.

Satan will often try to get in your ear and tell you "you are foolish," "you can't do that," "you're not equipped." Don't believe the lie! I'm thankful Gail did not believe the lies of Satan and charged him with the evil he is. Casa Agua Azul is rescuing children from his grasp because of Gail's willingness, the critical team behind Casa Agua Azul, and God's loving Holy Spirit!

—Your loving, admiring husband,
Ted Gordon

As you travel through the journey of reading this book, you will discover that obedience to God is very rewarding. God is wanting to use us to make a difference in this world. You can expect to see this in action as you keep on reading.

The work Gail is doing in my country is amazing. Seeing the children grow in Casa Agua Azul and how their lives are being changed at a young age is magnificent.

As a Guatemalan witnessing all the changes that are happening, it makes me so grateful to God for sending Gail to be a vessel to be used for enlarging his kingdom. How showing love in action can go a long way. Faith pleases God.

—Gaby Rogers
Volunteer at Casa Agua Azul

Reading this book was life-changing for me. Ms. Gordon is the "real deal"—her heart is devoted to God, and she's not afraid to show it. This book details her walk with the living God step by courageous step. She taught me many things I wasn't aware of before, and she also confirmed things I wasn't sure of in my own walk with Christ. In a very real way, she has taken me alongside her in these adventures and given me a deep look into her heart, the hearts of her colaborers, the hearts of the children, and the heart of Father God. I am forever grateful for my journey as a reader and fellow believer.

—Sylvia Maltzman
Blue Water Surrender Volunteer

After spending time at Casa Agua Azul, it was wonderful to read the story of its inception and Gail's incredible walk of faith. *A Trail of the Holy Spirit* will make you laugh, cry, and at times cringe as you learn about the complexities of Guatemalan culture and running a safe house. Gail has the patience of a saint and the tenacity of a lotus blossom. I am blown away by her strength and courage to overcome myriad obstacles and provide unending love to abused and abandoned Guatemalan children.

—Dr. Eileen Councill
Educational Consultant, School Leader, World Traveler

Love is the greatest gift that has the power to bring healing to all nations. *A Trail of the Holy Spirit* captivates our hearts as Gail shares her life story of God's divine purpose and vision brought to fulfillment by an act of obedience, tremendous faith, perseverance, and an unending ravishing love to bless and bring God's promises to the weak and broken children of Guatemala. Her personal experiences will ignite an intense yearning in your soul to "arise up out of the mundane" and declare, "More for you, God!" As ambassadors for Christ, I highly encourage anyone with a heartfelt desire to love beyond self, a hunger for missions, and defending the cause of the weak and fatherless to embrace the pages of this story. Prepare to be transformed, knowing that love never fails! So let's get rolling!

—Tabitha LaCourse

Foreword

Come on an adventure with Gail Gordon, or GG, as we like to call her. She has the vulnerability of someone "living within rainbows." You are either in love with her or you have not yet met her. I am honored to write the foreword for *A Trail of the Holy Spirit*. Gail is beautiful inside and out with the ability to find hope in brokenness that others may turn from. She is not interested in upending a culture but instead embraces it and its children.

So who is Gail Gordon?

When I first heard of the vision of Casa Agua Azul, I found myself asking the same thing. At the time, I was serving as the women's pastor at Great Lakes Dream Center based in Bay City, Michigan. The youth mission leader was sharing her mission experiences in Guatemala while meeting Gail and was already planning another trip back. I was captivated by the testimonies of love and faith with an eagerness in my spirit to hear more. Compelled to read *A Trail of the Holy Spirit*, I learned how God had placed an outpouring of love in Gail's heart, one that would take faith to bring love, hope, and healing to many vulnerable children in Guatemala. Saying yes to the vision with the Holy Spirit as the lead, the twists and turns cascaded into divine appointments taking her higher and deeper into the heart of God. With her husband, Ted, by her side, they embarked on a journey which blazed a trail into the jungle.

Her story carries immense power, and as I allowed myself to be immersed in her words, several quotes penetrated my heart and soul:

> Life is like a painting—it's not all sunny colors. (Chapter 5)

> I don't believe in renovating someone's culture but helping those suffering within it. (Chapter 7)

> When we allow God to come into our lives, his brilliance highlights and emphasizes the main object which he is expressing his love for—which is you. (Chapter 5)

GG's message challenges us to believe in not the seen but the unseen, to follow the light that comes from within and that which is deposited in your heart where faith lives. In part, her vision arose from an answer to her own mother's prayer: "God bless all the children in the world." The heartbeat passed on to her would one day become the children's home, Casa Agua Azul. Gail follows the light that God provides through his Son, Jesus Christ, with the driving force to live a life of love surrendered to God's will. Her desire, vision, and motivation propels her forward to enhance the many lives around her to draw them ever nearer to God. Knowing the risk, she has chosen to dedicate her life to making other lives better. She thinks outside of the box and teaches children to find new ways to celebrate everyday achievements. Through these lessons, they have gained inner strength despite the difficulty they have already faced. She is not only devoted to giving the children a home but also a safe place to heal.

Kingdom reality is experienced through the sharing of joy and accomplishments beyond what we can imagine. My heart was eager to visit Casa Agua Azul and personally meet the children, being a witness to faith realized. Upon arriving, as the gates opened, the children came running "head over heels" with the expression of pure joy to greet us. I could tell this was not just a mission house by the way Gail expressed her love to each child. Whether it was a pat on the back or a leaned-into hug, no child was left out. Just from the look on their faces and the way they were responding to her compassion, I could see a mutual affection of unconditional love expressed.

My hope for you as the reader is that you will get a chance to look through Gail's eyes as I did. Through the following pages in this book, you will see how she is tested in the fire and produces God's gold. A memorable quote when speaking of Casa Agua Azul: "It's not the building itself; it's what takes place within. It's a roof that protects and walls that shelter. As we place a roof over the children's heads, their hearts have a place to heal" (Chapter 5).

I recommend that you read this work without reservation, allowing God to teach you, through Gail's lesson, that faith also has its struggles. *A Trail of the Holy Spirit* gives hope to the many challenges one may face. We can move mountains as we listen and follow the Spirit of Truth. Through her, look at what happens when we trust deeply and are willing to cultivate a deposit of faith. Strength is given, perseverance gained. As we see step out, signs and wonders of promises are fulfilled.

—Pastor Kellie Dore

Introduction

A Trail of the Holy Spirit leads to Casa Agua Azul and is being written at the onset of the Coronavirus with many unknowns ahead for all. It is rather hard to write my story without God in it because God is my story. I am Gail Gordon, and this book is about my personal experience and the testimony of my faith along with many friends along the way. We are in this life together for one purpose—to glorify God. I believe we all have encounters with the living God; it's just that either we don't recognize it or we deny it as being real. God is real, and he cares to walk with us through this life and into the next. He says, "When my glory passes by, I will put you in a cleft in the rock and cover you with my hand until I have passed by" (Exodus 33:22 NIV). God is here now, and he is the same today as he was yesterday and will be forever. God has not changed, and his cry to the earth is that man will change, that man will come to him. For God so loves the world, and he continues to cry out to the world. I join hands with so many Old Testament prophets and utter, "I am here," in response to God's loving invitation.

Three perspectives from three generations represent the start of our story. There is great importance that the generations are not separated. We are knit together for a purpose. Who will carry out the next generation? If they are not taught and anointed with truth, we will merely all be lost children. Freedom will only be seen as a distant dream unless we unite. God's kingdom will advance in power and might as those who hold hands are united to bring forth what Christ has already given.

What is needed? Love! Love bonds, love heals, love is given, love protects. We must look deeper and touch the Spirit for transformation to occur, to break the cycle of abuse in order to bring forth the will of God. Poverty of spirit must go now in Jesus's name. God redeems, God loves, and God blesses.

The three generations of Casa Agua Azul are represented through

- Gail Gordon: American woman, founder of Casa Agua Azul, with no Spanish-speaking skills
- Gaby Rogers: a young Guatemalan woman raised by an American missionary
- Baby Gail Nahomy: a ten-week-old Guatemalan baby abandoned at birth.

1

The Hidden Crown

At such a time as this, we heard the news of "COVID-19, the Coronavirus." In light of this crisis, I was only able to imagine and wonder about baby Gail Nahomy, new in this world with all the chaos of a pandemic. I am concerned how this will affect her emotional and spiritual development in the future. As the days go by, the news and social media are displaying fear and more fear. It is March 14, 2020, close to one year since Casa Agua Azul received its first children. Casa Agua Azul is a children's home on the shore of Lake Izabal in the jungle of Guatemala. In a small indigenous village, baby Gail is peeking out through the mosquito net at just ten weeks old. She is the newest and youngest member of our Casa Agua Azul family.

Life is full of surprises! I, Gail Gordon, am the founder of Casa Agua Azul. I am known in the house as Mama Gail; in the village, I am known as "*Gringa*," or you may simply know me as GG. I'll answer all three with a smile. It was three months ago on January 31, 2020. I had looked at my cell phone and answered with a big question mark. The text was from Jerry and Griselda Makepeace, the house directors of Casa Agua Azul; it read, "And we are going to name our new baby Gail or Marie?" Mind you, the house accepts children only between the ages of three and thirteen years old. I was thinking, *I didn't know Griselda was pregnant. Who is this new baby, I wonder?* So naturally, I asked.

Griselda relayed that a young girl, eighteen years old, walked into the hospital and gave birth. She then took someone else's clothes and walked out! Her baby was born prematurely at seven months, weighing three pounds. The baby had no name and was completely abandoned by her birth mother.

The reasons why things like this happen often remain dark mysteries. CPS (Child Protective Services) searched for the mom, who had left with no trace. This was when the phone call from the hospital came to Casa Agua Azul, asking if we would care for the baby. Jerry and Griselda went to the hospital to investigate the situation and fell in love with the newborn baby. Jerry said to the hospital officials, "We agree to take the baby and give her a name and parents who will honor her humanity and, of course, love her. She is magnificently gorgeous." Jerry and Griselda named her Gail Nahomy.

This is why Casa Agua Azul exists. There are many vulnerable, abused, and abandoned children who need a safe refuge from the storms of life. They are innocent victims, hopelessly damaged; and if we don't fight for and defend them, who will? We are called to "defend the cause of the weak and the fatherless; uphold the cause of the poor and the oppressed" (Psalm 82:3 NIV).

I choose to believe God is a good God all the time, and he has a plan for our lives. So why the Coronavirus that is wreaking havoc across the earth? Why are children abused and abandoned so horrifically? These are good questions. There are many things on this side of heaven that I do not understand. God shows us in his Word that there are many untruths and half-truths in the world. The Coronavirus is just one of them. Beckah Shae defines the hidden crown as

> A fake crown which the enemy has placed upon his own head and declared himself king in this season. God wants us to know this attack is a lie and He is going to encircle His people against this attack. Do not fear! (https://www.facebook.com/beckahshae/photos/the-hidden-crown-i-have-some-really-great-news-for-you-today-god-has-a-hidden-cr/10158299408748729/?_rdr)

The Coronavirus is a real disease, but the fear it has produced is the problem. Fear is the lie that produces many more untruths. It is certain that fear will raise its ugly head, but we are called to rise above and to be ruled by love. Child abuse is not God's plan either. God says,

> It would be better to be thrown into the sea with a millstone tied around your neck than to cause one of these little ones to stumble. (Luke 17:2 NIV)

God is merciful and kind, but he is also just. Casa Agua Azul was established to be the loving arms of God present on the earth.

On March 14, 2020, I was flying back to Guatemala from Miami International Airport (MIA), which was in a lull as I entered. As I neared the security area, there was a mass of people wearing masks. Fortunately, the TSA line was empty. It was beautiful to just walk through with no wait. I felt sincerely blessed to be healthy and able to travel at this time. The flight I was on was close to empty. There were about thirty of us passengers, but the airline attendant said the return flight was fully booked. As I looked out over the clouds with the sunlight shining brightly, peace filled American Airlines Flight 2241 heading to Guatemala City. It was a beautiful day from above.

The reality of what was happening across the world was not fully known; it was just the beginning. Despite what was going on, faith led my heart, and I believed it was important that I traveled to Guatemala especially for the signing of necessary paperwork regarding Baby Gail. A newborn child without a registered name is in a vulnerable position to persons who could claim her for ill intentions. A family name carries a lot of weight in Guatemala; the custody of a child can depend upon his or her last name. Despite the urgent nature of my trip and the circumstances building around me, I felt confident that I was just doing business as usual and everything was okay. There was nothing blocking my path; all had been open doors with my husband and friends believing the same and urging me to go.

However, after landing in Guatemala, we were not allowed to deplane until we were checked by the Guatemalan medical team, which came aboard wearing masks and hazmat suits. My mind began to second-guess myself, sending me messages like, *Why am I here? The world is going crazy, and I am here in Guatemala alone.* So much for faith when weird reality sets in! I had been oblivious of the world situation up to this point, and I had to tell myself, *Go with the flow—I am here!*

After filling out some paperwork and having my temperature taken, I was allowed to disembark the plane and head to a series of checkpoints before reaching Customs. I walked past the crowd that had gathered from other arriving planes as many were waiting in long lines. Suddenly, I heard my name—"Gail!" I looked, and behold, there was a fellow missionary friend who had just arrived from Costa Rica. How is that for God making you feel comfortable in an unusual situation? We chatted for a while and eventually walked through the checkpoints together. Continuing to Customs, we found that it was empty again—no lines, just show your passport and keep on walking. There were no travelers present. I wondered where they all went because just a few baggage attendants were standing around. The baggage carousel area was quiet; it was an eerie feeling. About sixteen pieces of luggage were lined up by the still carousel, sitting in a dark shadow. It looked like a ghost town. I was definitely—defiantly—walking into a very unusual time. A worldwide state of emergency was coming into effect. The world at that moment appeared to be attacked by a stronghold of fear seeking to enter and dwell in our thought life. Communication between people is vital—we are in this world together, but what we are communicating makes the difference.

We are not made to live in isolation, which breeds fear and anxiety. I am grateful for wisdom and the efforts of governments, agencies, and individuals who are acting to protect us, but we are all called to stand and help those in need. Taking precautions to maintain good health is wise, but to hide in fear is of no use to the kingdom of light, which is God's place of peace and love for all mankind. Fear is a tool of darkness and is only coming to destroy. We have a choice. Fear is real, fear is a spirit, but we do not need to join forces with fear. We can align ourselves with wisdom, partnering in peace and perseverance for what God has planned for our lives. God's plan is simple: It is to prosper you in his kingdom. It is written:

> "For I know the plans I have for you," declares the Lord, "plans to prosper you and not to harm you, plans to give you a hope and a future." (Jeremiah 29:11 NIV)

It is by faith that we walk in his promises.

My faith is built on Jesus, and I write to you from this perspective. I am writing to share love, hope, joy, and peace with you. I have found Jesus is one who loves unconditionally. He offers living water at no cost. He offers love and kindness to all our fellow humans. I pray that the world will look and see who Jesus really is. His eyes have pleaded and continue to plead for all men to be with God.

The freedom that I walk in today has been a journey because through my thoughts and experiences, I filled myself with a false belief system. I built walls around my heart, which harmed me. My intentions were to protect myself, and this became a motivating factor in my life, the very fiber of my being. Whether consciously or unconsciously, it may very well have led to my own demise. I was totally unaware of the self-made prison I built. This prison was built from lies that I believed, untruths, unforgiveness, and events in my life which did not line up with the truth of God. I formed habits which became a method of operation with reactions all conveniently hidden in my attitudes and thought life.

The good news is that there is another way—the way of freedom. Our minds take us to dwelling places, whether positive or negative. Fortunately, we are able to build and fill our hearts with truth as written in God's Word (John 14:6). God's Word is not a rule book but a way to live the best life possible. We are able to dwell under the wing of the Almighty; his shadow is a safe place (Psalm 91). The kingdom of God is stronger than fear. In my spiritual darkness, Jesus became my rock and heartbeat. He was the one who had the power and authority to save me and give me life to the full. His truth is my living water, the water of life.

Let's get back to my story on March 14, 2020. I made it through the airport with flying colors. As I saw Jerry at the entrance, he was wearing his quintessential smile. "Welcome to Guatemala!" he exclaimed. Driving through Guatemala City turned into a series of traffic jams. Two accidents happened just a few minutes before our passing. Again, I was feeling blessed for being spared a terrible accident but still found my mind wrestling with two questions: *Why am I here, and what am I doing?* As Jerry and I drove on, we talked about the children at the house. Several of the children had been placed back with their families, and it was working out well for them. I love to hear stories of reconciliation! Also, at the same time, eight new children had been court-ordered to Casa Agua Azul. The situations they came from were heartbreaking. The violent abuse, abandonment, and neglect suffered by these children is hard to believe. It is clearly known and seen that hurt people hurt people and, in this case, their own children. Poverty on all levels is the culprit. Mankind is surely in need of a Savior, and none of us are exempt. The good news is despite the pain and injustice the children were suffering, I see Jesus healing their hearts. I have witnessed transformation before my eyes, and this will keep me going when the going gets tough. It is worth the good fight of faith.

Finally, we arrived at Casa Agua Azul. It had been fourteen hours since leaving my home during the onset of the Coronavirus. I was greeted by seventeen excited children, half of whom I had not met yet. The hugs and love flowed from the delight within the children. It had been two and a half months since I was there with my precious angels, and I love them all the same. They are happy, but you can see in their faces the need for love; there is still a hollowness of the past.

Thinking about life and the terrible things that happen, you may be angry at God and blaming God for many things. Horrific things happen in life. I see it right here in front of my eyes. Who would beat a child to the point that the child is hospitalized for five days for not selling five bags of chips, which amount to less than $15?

God is not the only player in this world. Bad things are all around us every day. Often we blame God for man's actions. God still wants to be our friend no matter what we say about him. He loves us regardless. He wants to take the pain from our hearts and make all things right.

There are so many questions in my mind. What can I change, and how can I do it? I believe we all need to take a closer look at life and at death. I know that I certainly do. Is it possible to open our minds enough to realize that they may need to be changed? Is there possibly a need to look at some things differently—and a little more deeply—before we point our fingers at others and blame? Our feelings do not always direct us to the right place. Am I a terrible person because there are so many times my mind and my feelings have been wrong about something, someone, God, or myself? I say no. We are humans living in a human condition which is not perfect, but the question is *Am I willing to be changed?* We change the sheets on our beds. We change the color of paint on our houses, so maybe I need to change in some areas within. I must ask myself, "Am I able to put down my pride and walk in humility, to be honest, to give my heart to God and allow his love to change what I am not able, to trust him a little deeper?"

My first day back in Guatemala had been very exciting. As the sun set, I discovered my return flight home was canceled. The email said to reschedule. Okay! So I pressed the link to read: "No flights available." I chuckled to myself. My mind went back to this virus, which was shutting down life as we knew it, and we had no idea for how long; the hidden crown was revealing itself through the Coronavirus, working tirelessly to create panic, fear, and to threaten our freedom.

This false crown is in conflict with the True Crown, and a war was being waged in both the physical and spiritual realm. My mind is directed to thinking about war, to those who have protected our country and have given their lives for the freedom we have. Freedom did not come without a price. The soldier at some point had to take a step in faith, knowing he may be harmed to the point of losing his life. In faith, the soldier prepared himself with a helmet to protect his head, his mind, ammunition to wage war against the enemy, and obedient trust in his superior officers. The soldier walked in wisdom, made ready for what is ahead. Hiding will not win the victory—at some point, each person will have to stand like a soldier unless they choose to lie down and die. Victory is taken, not given, and there is a chance you will get hit by a bullet along the way, but by fighting, wearing the helmet of salvation, walking in wisdom, and carrying the word of truth dripping in love, you will tear down the stronghold of fear (Ephesians 6). The ultimate victory and freedom I have found are in Jesus.

I have found my answer to why I am here. I am a soldier on a journey with Jesus; every day I prepare for battle. My greatest companions are faith and trust. I may not know the specifics at the moment, but it is important that I am here, and it is important that you too are here. You may be the light someone else needs to see.

At times on this journey, I have felt lost, but God has always sent others to be by my side.

Light comes from many beautiful sources. The most beautiful light is the light of Jesus, which shines through people as they act and speak in love. As a missionary, you can plan great things like a wonderful team joining you, but not everything goes as expected—that is for sure! I was so delighted to have Gaby join me that week in Guatemala as the Coronavirus continued to multiply and wreak havoc. Gaby is my friend, and she is the daughter of a great missionary friend of mine, Riechelle Rogers, whom I call Mother Theresa of Guatemala City. We met many years ago on a cell phone call before Casa Agua Azul was even a thought in my mind. Luis, my Guatemalan mission partner at the time, said to me, "Here, say hi. She is an American." This is a habit of my friend Luis, awkward at times but on this occasion very fruitful. During this time, I was leading mission teams to Casa Hogar Achiam, a home for children in the Peten region of Guatemala. That phone call was the beginning of a valuable relationship. Riechelle, with her connections, made it possible for two of the young boys at the home to receive eye surgery, changing their lives. I love how God works and brings people together. We did not meet in person until quite a while later. I was staying at a hotel in the Rio Dulce between mission teams.

A TRAIL OF THE HOLY SPIRIT

I helped her rescue three young girls who were being sexually molested, and that was also when I first met Jerry Makepeace, who is now our house director! He was our getaway driver who safely transported the girls away from their situation to the police station, where they could be processed and taken to a safe house in another part of Guatemala. The magnitude of children suffering was being shown to me.

On day two during the beginning of the pandemic, life was filled with more unknowns. Jerry and I were out and about, running errands as usual. Jerry and I spent the morning in Puerto Barrios at our lawyer's office. The prearranged plan was to sign the necessary papers for baby Gail Nahomy, but little did we know that court was just canceled until the president opened it back up. Once again, that question came to mind: *Why am I here?* It seemed that the plans for the last seven to ten years and not just for today kept getting changed. As Jimmy Greenfield, an old friend of mine, would say, "Don't fight the river even if there are rocks ahead. Don't fight the river!" Okay, I decided, I am not going to fight the river, just ride it out in faith.

As lunch time rolled around and passed, I could not imagine what would happen next. We decided to go to the mall, which was quite empty. It was strange and funny at the same time that we decided to eat at the Chinese restaurant. Again, don't you just love how God works? As we sat there, talking about China and why there was hardly anyone in the mall, guess who walked by but the judge from court which had been canceled. After engaging him in polite conversation about our predicament, he agreed it was a good idea to sign the papers, but I wondered when that would happen because the court was closed indefinitely! It was great that we were in agreement, but after he left, we still had no solution. By now you might start to wonder because this all sounds a little crazy—and it is crazy! That is why I am constantly asking myself the same question over and over. I have found myself feeling very alone in Guatemala on many occasions in strange situations. It sure would help if I spoke Spanish! For some reason, I believed God had called me to start a children's home in Guatemala, and this is just how it rolls. You don't fight the river of the Holy Spirit. We must continue to walk by faith and trust God at all times—good and bad, whether the world is shutting down rather quickly or not. His plan is perfect.

As evening approached, we were excited to pick Gaby up at the bus stop in downtown Rio Dulce. Gaby arrived on the *Litegua* bus line, but none of us knew she was on the last bus in, and there were none going out for who knows how long just like the song "Hotel California": "You can check out any time you like, but you can never leave!" I attributed these unexpected events to the hidden crown of Corona. I have been convinced from the beginning that we will learn much from God during this season, which has become a very unusual adventure on the planet.

Jerry, Gaby, and I found ourselves walking around in a daze in the *Supermercado*, La Torre. People were starting to wear face masks. Unlike America, there was toilet paper on the shelves as well as hand sanitizer. When we saw Jerry's friend, the district attorney, in the store, he shared with us that the airports were shutting down in Guatemala. This was when it all started to click for me. Something was going on there. Gaby looked at her phone. We were still in the store as the Monday night 8:00 p.m. news broadcast from President Alejandro Giammattei was on. He stated, "All public transportation is being canceled, stores are being closed, agencies and employment will not be functioning for twenty-one days." After arriving just one hour ago, Gaby was questioning, "Did I make the right decision on coming here?" Little did she know that I was thinking the same thing, and Jerry was just smiling from ear to ear.

After checking our groceries, Gaby said, "I feel like I am living a story told by a little kid where the kid is saying, 'There is a flu that is going around. There is no toilet paper anywhere because we just bought the last of it. The schools are canceling classes because this flu is going around the world. The adults are going crazy, and I don't know why they keep saying the flu is going around the world.'"

As we left the store, I looked in the shopping cart, and I was amazed and slightly embarrassed by all the toilet paper Jerry had bought. We want you to know we were not hoarding it; we were just using forward thinking. We had seventeen children at Casa Agua Azul, and three were in diapers, for a possible twenty-one days of no escape. Once again, I heard the melody of the song "Hotel California." Being from the Florida Keys, all I could think of was what you do when a hurricane is coming.

Outside the store, the ATM wouldn't give any money to foreign cards. Reality was starting to hit. The gas tank was now reading empty. I guessed it was time to pray; it certainly was an exciting day and was not letting up.

God really pulls things together in mysterious ways. After this crazy day, while we were driving home in the dark, we prayed for wisdom. You can't go wrong with wisdom, and we needed a lot of wisdom. As we entered through the gate of Casa Agua Azul, the stars were brilliant in the darkness. We were greeted with love and hugs. The children were bursting forth with an overwhelming joy, which was contagious! They were eager to carry in the supplies and our bags. A candle lit up the room, and more sleepy children staggered starry-eyed to give more hugs as they wandered about in a dream state, still half asleep. Gaby headed for the shower but never made it past her bed on the second floor of the house. I guess she was extremely tired, and maybe I was feeling a little jealous to still be awake. My heart wanted to see baby Gail before I rested for the night. I had rocked and prayed for her for a few hours in the early morning. She is the most precious little thing—like a China doll—so tiny but strong. I peeked into her room, and she was awake, so I tiptoed in and picked her up. I noticed she was very hot, most definitely running a fever. Blanca, one of our great nannies, tended to her along with Jerry and me in the medical room. We were about to rush her to the hospital in Puerto Barrios, a drive of over two hours away, when Dr. G called to save the night. Dr. G is a wonderful doctor. He is one of our team members who is available to us twenty-four-seven. Baby Gail was in so much pain from an intestinal infection which had grabbed ahold of her. I could only think about her life and what she has already gone through in just weeks, which was her entire life. Her tears became my tears, and that was when in my heart she became my child.

By 2:30 a.m., Baby Gail and all of us were snug in our beds at Casa Agua Azul. As I rested for the night, I remembered sitting in the office of CNA (National Council of Adoption, the agency which oversees children's affairs) with Gaby two years prior, praying that all the paperwork was finally in order. I was exasperated—there really was nothing left within me, but I was going to fight until the end. Gaby said, "Gail, I believe you are going to have your orphanage soon." This pierced my heart! I almost fell out of the chair to cry in the fetal position while in the waiting room of the government office in Guatemala City. I believed Gaby's words wholeheartedly, but I was so beaten down by the process, the fight, the waiting, and the many struggles which had been going on for years. As I lay in bed this night, I marveled at the victory God had carved out of our efforts and his mercy.

All I can say about this undertaking is how great is our God. I think of the words from the song "Amazing Grace" about the God "who saved a wretch like me. I once was lost, but now I see." It is the mercy, the grace of God, walked out in faith, relying on the true hidden crown of Christ on the cross. The crown of thorns carries the weight of the world and has all authority here on earth as it is in heaven. It is the power of his Holy Spirit rising up for justice; truly God is good all the time. He takes what the devil means for harm and turns it for good. Not one minute of your life is a waste when you look to the King of kings. He redeems from death and destruction and gives life to the full. You are a jewel in his crown! All you need to do is believe. Oh, how God loves faith. I testify to this. He is my testimony—look what Christ has done. To him be all glory, for he is worthy of all our praise. He who started a good work in me will bring it to completion, and he will do the same for you.

There is a dream in your heart created for you that is meant to be lived. Look in your heart; what do you see? What do you feel? What do you dream? Do not be afraid. God says, "Be strong and courageous," for God did not give us a spirit of fear but one of power, love, and a sound mind (2 Timothy 1:7 NKJV). This is truth. Grab onto the river of life. It is here, it is flowing, and it is free. Casa Agua Azul, once a vision and a dream, is a living reality today to bless the many children in need.

This is why I am here.

A TRAIL OF THE HOLY SPIRIT

Gaby and baby gg

2

The American

Have you ever stopped, taken a look at your life, and wondered how you got there? My journey to Guatemala is much like that. It started in 2007 while sailing with my family and spending hurricane season in the Rio Dulce where the jungle is thick. There is something about the jungle and her people that lures you in as creation speaks. It captivates my soul. Your eyes become filled with monstrous green vegetation while the sound of a symphony conducted in natural sounds, all unique in themselves, creates a song of beauty, but Guatemala is also one of the hottest places I have ever been. Sweat would just drip off my face! I'm sure you can imagine me asking myself *How did I get here?* nearly every time I wiped my face!

As I think back, I see that a thread in this tapestry was being woven many years prior. My husband had spent time in the historic colonial city of Antigua, Guatemala, in his teens. His family owned a home within the city limits, where we later shared our honeymoon, looking out to Volcán de Agua. The area of Antigua is mountainous terrain and much cooler than the Rio Dulce. At one time, Antigua was the capital of Guatemala; today it is a popular travel destination. Bright colors flash from every direction, intoxicating your senses. Whispers of ruins and cobblestone roads seep into your core, diffusing the sensation of days past. The Hotel Casa Santo Domingo and Museum is a powerful element of that sensation. Dating back to 1538, it was once a monastery which was destroyed in the 1773

Santa Marta earthquake. The hotel was built on the grounds of that monastery. Today the city of Antiqua is filled with artifacts, art, fine food, and comfortable accommodations. The entire country is extraordinarily beautiful—from the Pacific coast through the mountains and all the way over to the Caribbean Sea where the Rio Dulce lies. Beauty is all around us no matter where we are in the world. I believe there is a plan and purpose for each person's life unique to each one, and because of that beauty, it is to our great excitement to discover the answer to the question "How did I get here?"

During the Corona quarantine in Guatemala, I was starting to be called "*La Americana*" (the American). I wasn't sure I liked my new title. It scared me a little because I had to be cleared medically twice by the health officials. The first time in the airport as I landed in Guatemala City was understandable, but then the Rio Dulce Clinic officials called, looking for "the American." Someone reported that an American was in the village, so they wanted to check me out for the virus. Public transportation was shut down, so I was asked to drive to the clinic, which is forty-five minutes away. Jerry drove me in. After more paperwork and shining the light on my forehead again, I was cleared. I felt like I was in the scene of a movie. I am thinking of *ET*—I want to go home, but the reality is more like "Hotel California" again. Next, the officials from the El Estor Medical Clinic proceeded to hunt me down. I am glad I was not at the house because if they took me away, that would be really scary! I decided to carry a book with my glasses just in case because I would go stir crazy mad with nothing to do. Anyone suspected to have the virus is taken to Guatemala City and put in quarantine in a special hospital for a month or so—or so they said at that time. The public hospitals here are not what an American is accustomed to. It would take a little bit of an adjustment to settle in, and not speaking the language would make it even more challenging unless you are good at charades, then I guess you would have fun. Again, I hear in my mind Jimmy's voice saying, "Don't fight the river," then Gaby saying, "Don't be a salmon and swim upstream!" Right, it's not going to work out too well because if they want to take you away, they are going to take you away! Just surrender!

How many times do you wake up in moments of your life and wonder what is going on? Mystery awaits; looking out from the mosquito net is the story of Casa Agua Azul. No one knows where the wind comes from, and no one knows where the wind blows to (John 3:8).

One day, on the shore of Lake Izabal, two years after sailing into the Rio Dulce, prayer broke forth. It was an unusually cold day in February 2013, and the Holy Spirit spoke, echoing loudly across the water. The sky was misty, pelting down small droplets of rain. Gray was painted across the sky, yet something was being held back. It was dark, yet it was light. Crashing waves bore witness as they beat on the shore. The wind blew with great force. While I stood looking out across the water, the clouds formed a line across the horizon with a voice utterly hidden yet speaking as the mountains roared. The whole earth groaned as words poured forth. I felt a strength greater than myself being reinforced through agreement by Luis on my left and Mary, my mission friend, on my right. We felt the mightiness of God in his presence. Together we began to pray. Words and details came in an ethereal way. God was speaking forth a plan the way a waterfall brings forth endless water. The property on which we stood carries peace like no other; by the plan and will of God, the house contains a story written before the beginning of time. I listened and looked while the cloud over the house appeared as a dream, one with a desire aching for life, to bring heaven down to earth. The cry is the heart of God for the children. Ten years after hearing that cry, I looked out from the mosquito net and walked down to the shore where a time spent in prayer coincided with the opening of heaven's gate.

Time has an ebb and flow. What you see in your mind can take time to materialize in the physical realm. That is what happened in June 2019; I was standing on the same shore, but this time, I was watching eleven children bathing, filled with laughter and life. What once was a mere abstract dream, a thought empowered by prayer, is here!

Traveling back and forth between Islamorada, Florida, and Guatemala for so many years has become my norm, but it also creates a big blur. Where is home? My husband is in Florida, my son out on the sea, my parents are aging, and my life has become a living rectangle between Connecticut, Florida, the Bahamas, and Guatemala. It's said that home is where your heart is; on my journey, I have many places I call home, so I visit them all. Love compels your heart because that is who you are. What lives within your heart is what will shine forth.

One night, while in Guatemala City, I was sleeping under the moon, and it became very hypnotic as the light of God's promise was shining over the city. While watching the clouds pass overhead, I started pondering the days to come and reflecting on the days past. In the crisp air, the wind was constantly moving the clouds, revealing the once-hidden beauty of a star-filled sky, with the city light backdrop looming in the distance. How can one not wonder at the majestic beauty of God? Urban camping is not the same as sailing the open ocean, yet it has its own allure of unexplainable secrecy just begging to reveal the unknown.

Little did I know what I was getting into when I said *yes* to the Lord so many years ago about building a children's home in a foreign land. I remember the night clearly. In 2013, I was living aboard our sailboat *Adonai* in the Florida Keys with my wonderful husband, Ted, who is my greatest advocate. I awoke in the night—one of many restless nights fighting with the Lord, or maybe I was fighting with myself. Nevertheless, they were sleepless nights! What I do know is I did not sleep but for moments. My mind was questioning. For nearly two years, I tossed and turned with the question *Are you calling me, Lord?* I had only a few years under my belt as a believer, and I was very enthusiastic to serve the Lord. My occupation at that time was that of a mom, a hairdresser, and coming alongside my husband's fence contracting business. That memorable night, I woke up, and I felt like Jacob in the Bible as if God broke my hip. I relented. I gave up the fight even though a fighter I am to the core. I then thought to myself, *I do not want to be Jonah in the belly of a whale and get spewed out!* It is important that I do my best to build a home for the abandoned and abused children of Guatemala. That is a *Whoa!* place to be—no thank you. Fear has its benefits when it is fear of God! So how could I say *no* to God out of fear about the mission? Because "perfect love casts out fear" (1 John 4:8), I was able to say *yes!*

God is a loving Father who is good all the time. Many events brought me to this place by the sovereign hand of a loving God who is constantly seen at work when one looks. Seek and you shall find love without measure. All of us have a story written in a book in heaven which existed way before the beginning of time. God is a timeless, ever-present Father who loves his children unconditionally. He is mysterious, kind, and present. He is heard in the still small voice; he is the light in your eyes; he is omnipresent.

I don't remember a lot of the days in my life, but there is one I do clearly. It was fall in the year 2005. I was living in my dream home, with my dream family and my dream American life. Our house was on an airstrip overlooking a marina in the Florida Keys. Our business was prosperous, and the real estate market was booming! Before marrying my husband, Ted, we both had experienced on our own, separately, what it is like to be homeless and penniless. The dream we were living was beyond our wildest imaginations at one point in time. When I was pregnant with our son Trevor, we borrowed $400 to buy a truck—one side of which was smashed in entirely. I climbed over the stick shift every day without complaining, and I was quite happy. This was the beginning of many blessings to come. Regardless of the situation, every good gift comes from above, poured out by the Father of Lights. The question is are you willing to let go of your preconceived ideas and receive the next good gift? This was a lesson I had to learn.

On that unforgettable day, my husband called out to me from our downstairs office—"I found our boat!"

I said to myself, *Yeah right, whatever. Just call me Miss Positive here. We both are dreamers, and here is another one.*

Not so this time! He was serious. Ted always desired to take our son Trevor sailing when he became an adolescent. Ted had lived aboard with his father in Saint Thomas when he was in his teens and always wanted to give this gift to our son—to take him out of our society in these crucial years of growing up. The many temptations in our culture easily led our children astray into the world of drugs and alcohol and so much more. It was difficult to see how we could ever afford to do this, but on that day, he could. We were going to let go of everything and go sailing! *Sailing*! I was not so sure about this. I love to go windsurfing, but I am afraid of being seasick. At one time I had dreamed of sailing, but it was a long-forgotten dream.

I said "Okay, I will give it a try. I'm not sure, but I will give it a try."

The next day, I also remember because Ted said, "Let's go talk to Lisa." She is our neighbor who is in real estate. He said, "Let's talk to her about putting the house on the market."

Reluctantly, again, I said, "Okay."

We walked down the airstrip to Lisa's house and shared with her that we were thinking of selling our house—and that was it. I am not so certain we shared with our son the good news yet—that we would be taking him away from all his friends in high school and he would be alone with his parents on a sailboat, homeschooling! Doesn't that sound like fun for a teenager? The next morning, a knock on the door came; it was Jay and Lisa.

"We want to buy your house." *What!* How can one answer so fast? We were just going to list it! Soon after, Ted, Trevor, and I flew down to Puerto Rico to look at this sailboat my husband says is ours, the one he saw on the Internet. The boat's name was *Reef Shark*, owned by Scully, a writer, and his wife. *Reef Shark* was a forty-seven-foot catamaran made in South Africa by Voyage Yachts, sitting in dry dock at Puerto Del Rey Marina in Fajardo, Puerto Rico.

The hardest day of my life was next—to sign on the dotted line. If we did not let go, I would not be here now in Guatemala. It had to be faith and trust in God, definitely not in myself! We renamed *Reef Shark* and made a family agreement to go for it with no regrets. We gave the boat the name *Gabriella* because it was the feminine form of Gabriel, the angel who carried messages of powerful good news, whom my mom named me after. The translation from Hebrew is "God is my strength."

Everything we owned we either sold it, threw it away, or gave it away—anything which would not fit in our catamaran. I no longer wanted the beautiful American dream which we received though

God's blessing and hard work by keeping our hands to the plow. Something greater was stirring in my heart. I wanted the kingdom dream, the wind of the Holy Spirit. Where the wind blows to and where it comes from, no one knows (John 3:8). It's interesting that God works that way in our lives. My husband and I were willing to give up our business, but in my heart, I felt God say, "Thank you for putting it in my hands, and now I want to give it back to you differently." Wisdom spoke to my husband differently yet with the same result. I was feeling so uprooted as the Florida Keys have always been my home and dear to my heart. I couldn't understand why I wanted to leave what I loved so much. What was always home was being dislodged from my heart.

We prepared our sailing vessel *Gabriella* for over a year, doing our part to make her seaworthy. In June 2007, we pulled the anchor and set sail with a couple of friends—Lisa, Natalie, and my father-in-law Bill. Our plan was to sail through Central America down to Panama, to cross over into the South Pacific, and work our way toward New Zealand and Australia. Our motto was "Don't look back, and have no regrets!" This was a great adventure that I'll cherish in my heart forever. One of the greatest blessings was that my husband and I watched our son grow from a boy into a man.

When you are out to sea for long periods of time, it is hard *not* to hear God. Nature has a fury and, if anything, will humble you. Mother Nature will do it with raging seas. We are definitely not in control of the universe. On the ocean, there is a lot of time to reflect and ponder *Why are we here?* That question again! In between times of reflection, there are serious responsibilities while out at sea especially on a long crossing where no land is in sight for weeks. Standing watch at night to look out for ships and storms needs to be taken seriously.

Fortunately, I love to spend time under the night sky, looking up at the brilliance of the stars. One of my favorite views is when the sea becomes glass-calm, and the night sky reflects in the sea. At times like that, there is no horizon; sea and sky become one. This doesn't happen very often, but when it does, it's really special. At night, as the sun would go down, we would always trim our sails. If a storm comes up at night, you want to be prepared because storms will often blow in quickly. I have seen the radar go totally black, which is not a good feeling because then, you can't see any ships that may be out there, and you are about to get hit by a big storm. I prayed one night as I was watching a blackout, and before my eyes, the blackness on the radar split, and a path was made for us in the dark of night! There is a God who is in control, and that God is not us.

Another very memorable instance of God's intervention at sea was when we were just off the coast of Niue, the smallest island country in the South Pacific. When we were changing night watch shifts one night, all three of us were up—Ted, Trevor, and myself. I was inside, and I heard this ear-splitting noise as if I were inside of a drum. The whole boat shook. My son and husband were outside as they saw a storm approach. As quickly as it came, it left. A waterspout had hit our boat, tearing up the jib, which is the front sail, shredding it and twisting it to pieces. However, our mast was still standing! After the shock wore off, almost all was well—except for the need to find a new sail out in the middle of the sea!

Another serious sailing story happened offshore at Nicaragua. My husband was on night watch on a windy night, blowing around twenty knots. For some reason, he didn't wake us up or let us know what was going on until the morning. He had quite the night as the rest of us all slept like babies. There are times where you need to just act fast, and this was one of them. He noticed that a boat in the distance was on the same course as we were. Every time he changed course, the other boat would match our course. Ted described the situation as the boat playing some type of "chicken" with us. This went on for a while; eventually, the other boat gained ground on us. It was a much larger boat, a fishing vessel of some type. Ted saw the bow almost upon us. They were going to ram us, starboard side midship. Ted quickly jibed *Gabriella*, which in a heavy wind is able to break your boom. Thankfully, the boom remained unharmed. With the power of the wind and God's favor, we were able to outrun the vessel.

Sailing is beautiful, and I love it. The wind, the freedom, the sunrise and sunset, God's hand at work constantly painting beauty, with the wonders of nature revealing themselves as his magnificent handiwork—the wonders never cease. While leaving the Galapagos, we saw so much sea life. There was a pod of porpoise—hundreds of them were jumping and swimming all about. We couldn't take our eyes off them until the pod of whales showed up. There was some competition for our attention, all stunning beauty!

By now after all these sailing stories, you may wonder how Guatemala fits into this picture. After we left the Florida Keys and explored Mexico and Belize, we spent four months waiting out hurricane season in Rio Dulce, Guatemala. Mario's Marina became our home on the river while we were there. This is where I met Kevin, a three-year-old boy who absolutely stole my heart. I would walk in the remote village of Esmeralda behind the Marina, and Kevin would stand outside his diminutive house every day and wave with the biggest smile, wearing his little red T-shirt. He was my first friend, and then there was Karla, a seven-year-old pastor's daughter. She too would smile and wave. Kevin lived on the outskirts of Esmeralda; his family was Q'eqchi' (descendants of the Maya) and they all worked at the *finca*, which means "farm" in Spanish. His mom would watch me every day like a hawk and never wave.

After walking in the village for some time, I realized that at the end of town, I was being watched. Many of the mothers would bring their children inside their huts when they saw me. Lisa was with me one day, and we both noticed this, not understanding at first. At that time, there was a lingering belief among the people that Americans would steal children for body parts. This was especially true in the outer regions. Before we had arrived in Guatemala, an American couple up in the mountains were killed for that very reason. They say ignorance is bliss! While out on my walks to make friends, I took time to feed the animals along the way and take photos. Then I would print out the photos on my boat. This was before cell phone photo galleries. When I walked by the next day, I would share them with the families. Eventually, trust was built, and friendships started. Before I left Guatemala, I was doing family portraits for many in the neighborhood. It was nice to be able to give them something special.

In October 2007, when we left the Rio Dulce, I really cried. Before we left, I had met Luis at a swap meeting at Mario's Marina, selling his art wares. He was recently back in Guatemala from a long stay in California. Luis is Guatemalan and bilingual. Little did I know at that time he would become my partner to help build Casa Agua Azul, a home for abandoned and abused children, a dream I didn't even know existed at that time. It was the farthest thing from my mind. Actually, it wasn't even in my mind or my realm of being. Luis became my new friend along with Karla. They were instrumental in helping us get little Kevin and his cousin Anna Marie enrolled in school. Lack of funds for books and school uniforms was holding them back. I wasn't aware of the cultural split at that time between the indigenous Q'eqchi and the Hispanic culture.

As I look back, I can see that the two communities, although living side by side, didn't appear to socialize very much. The Q'eqchi lived on the outskirts of town in their own small village area. Since then, I have learned much. I have read about the brutal civil war, a thirty-six-year war from 1960 to 1996. When I ponder this, I realize many of the elders in Guatemala lived through this horrific time, and the memories are faded but fresh. The Izabal region was reported as having some of the worst massacres. This is the area we are in. Luis and Karla are of Hispanic descent. In a spiritual sense, I see them bridging a gap in the cultures, alleviating pain so that healing can continue. God sees us all the same, but on earth, due to pain, we tend to have separations. Now throw an American in the mix, and things can get really crazy. I also learned that putting Kevin in school could jeopardize his parents' jobs with the *finca* owners. Uneducated people become a source of cheap labor for the *finca* owners. In return, the owners provide a family with a dwelling space and a means of food which they would not have otherwise. Life is complex. There are no easy answers, and so I cried.

Leaving Guatemala was a big lesson in letting go of more of what I love, but by releasing and opening my hands, I have experienced many other things that I love. I see life as a succession of letting go. You see, if I never let go, I wouldn't be here where I am today. As humans, we have a tendency to grab hold and clench our fists around what we love. True love is freedom that is held with an open hand.

Moving on across the sea, I had a great time with my family. We stopped in Honduras, then we bought shrimp off a shrimp boat in Nicaragua behind a tiny island hiding from the intense wind while celebrating my fiftieth birthday. In the sky that day, the sunset appeared to go on for hours. Exploring the Caribbean Islands of Kuna Yala, Panama, was one of my favorite stops. Sailing through the Panama Canal revealed some of the greatest work of man's hands, a history lesson in itself. We then stopped in the Las Perlas Islands in Panama. Here some people really do fly their dirty laundry to the mainland to be cleaned. We had some laundry washed and learned why. The island's fresh water shortage makes it very expensive, similar to the prices charged in a grand hotel. From there, we ventured over to the Galapagos Islands, taking us nine days to arrive at the port. The next leg of our trip would be a twenty-one-day sail offshore.

We arrived in the South Pacific, landing in the Marquesas. When I saw the palm trees, which were extraordinarily tall, I could not hold back tears from my eyes. The sight was so beautiful after seeing only blue for three weeks. Then we all saw a truck, and I pointed to it like a three-year-old child, stuttering, "The truck!" I can't explain it—maybe you can—but you have to try it. Spending so many days at sea is a physical challenge, but more so it's a mental challenge. In the end, you receive a great reward; perseverance will get you through what seems like forever. If you think you are feeling isolated during the Coronavirus, I can relate. We would watch airplanes fly over and say, "Oh, twelve-hour flight, no problem. Try sailing." What is a long time? Ask a sailor.

I don't know what was more beautiful—Tahiti, Mo'orea, Bora Bora, or the Cook Islands, where at last I heard the English language spoken outside of my family or cruisers for the first time in almost a year. My favorite island in the South Pacific is Niue. The name means "coconut," and it is the smallest island country in the world. Her mother country is New Zealand. Unless you are sailing there, you will need to fly to New Zealand first. Niue is home to the sea snake, which the locals call "Kind Katuali." The sea snake is abundant there like no other place. They are actually deadly poisonous, but their teeth are set way back in their mouth, and they are not able to open up wide enough to penetrate your skin. I was nervous about them at first especially when my son stepped on one. You get used to the snakes, and then they start to look like pretty ribbons in the sea. A funny moment happened one day while I was taking a movie of them in the water. They became attracted to the shining reflection of my camera and started coming toward the camera and not leaving. Naturally, I freaked out. The camera clip was going round and round, sounding like I was being eaten by the snakes.

Somewhere in our travels, when my husband went home to check on business, he decided to list our boat for sale; this was earlier than we had planned. He figured it would take at least a year to sell. We received a phone call almost immediately, which is unheard of during the decline of economy in the United States in 2008. This crazy couple from California saw the boat on the Internet, just like Ted and I did, and believed it was their boat! The interest in our vessel caused us to hurry along to Tonga, which was an experience in itself.

Tonga is between Niue and Fiji. The culture is so different from the rest of the South Pacific. It is common for men to wear long skirts. We called them "man skirts," but there is a proper name for them which I have forgotten. My son, who is so confident in his manhood, purchased his own man skirt, and he looked very handsome. Another outfit I saw was a man wearing a handwoven straw mat wrapped around his waist. For a belt, he had a piece of rope with some large conch shells hanging off it. It was interesting. We didn't stay long in Tonga because we had to get to Fiji.

We met the prospective buyers, Todd and Renee, in Fiji. They brought a surveyor with them who loved surfing. The survey took place on a sandbar, and when we were finished, we sailed out to the reef to go surfing! Todd really wanted to marry his bride, Renee, aboard *Gabriella* in California in just a couple of months. Negotiations began—another lesson of letting go of my heart because Gabriella had become my home. We agreed on a price and a closing date. As I said, Todd wanted the boat in California, so my husband said to him, "Todd, it is actually better to sail around the world to get to California than to go from Fiji by way of Hawaii to California."

Being a rugged rock climber, he wasn't taking our suggestion. He was up for the challenge. Todd ended up hiring us to sail the boat because as a new captain, he was not able to get insurance approval for such a crossing. We still needed a more experienced crew to meet insurance regulations. I emailed a friend of mine who was a very experienced sailor in the racing circuit.

I said, "Hey Janet, how would you like to sail from Fiji to California?"

Of course, she asked, "When?"

Naturally, I said, "Next week."

Her schedule just happened to be open, and she accepted the challenge.

It took us more than two weeks to get out of Fiji because the wind was blowing so hard, a steady thirty-five knots plus a current against us. We were not able to make headway and get out of the channel to enter the ocean. The wind never let up! But finally, we were on our way, sailing as close to dead upwind as a catamaran can go, which is not too close! Aboard *Gabriella* were Ted, Trevor, Renee, Todd, Janet, and myself. It was so rough that we were hoping to hit the doldrums around the equator, where we would be able to motor upwind and make our tack. It never happened—the wind never let up. Ted was thinking seriously that we might need to sail to the Aleutian Islands of Alaska to tack back and make Hawaii. That would be a seriously long tack!

Along the way, we missed making ground at American Samoa where we hoped to stop for a break. Then we were not able to make the Line Islands, but on the outskirts, we were able to pull in off Kiribati; this is where it is thought that Amelia Earhart crashed her plane in July 1937. This island is pristine and untouched, surrounded by a coral reef. There is always a glow in nature when man has been absent. We anchored just outside of the reef so that we wouldn't damage either the boat or the reef. Trevor and Todd swam in; I followed on a surfboard while my husband kept the boat safely off the shore and the surrounding reef, which came up to the shoreline.

My son got on the island ahead of me and said, "Mom, keep paddling."

I asked "Why?"

And he just said, "Mom, just keep paddling."

I finally got to the shore, then he told me that a giant sea turtle came out from under the reef and chased off a shark that was coming at him! Okay, wow, what else can you say but "This island is beautiful, and we were still under God's protection in this remote place." But eventually, we would have to paddle back out. After exploring the island, my son got in the water first while I was afraid, standing on the shore alone. I was having trouble getting on the surfboard and off the reef. My son was so kind—he just kept treading water and waiting for me. I didn't know that the sharks were bumping him and Todd this whole time. We reached the boat, and as soon as we got onboard, my husband was reeling in a big fish; but suddenly, we all heard and felt a great *chunk*! The only thing left on the line was the fish head. A shark had come by and cut that big fish right off. *Reality check!* We had to move on since there was no safe anchorage here.

We continued sailing. The sky had been gray for weeks. The wind was still blowing thirty-five-plus knots and not letting up. We had not seen even one airplane in the sky or any sea life below except for the sharks off Kiribati. I noticed Renee was very nervous on her night watch, so I started keeping watch with her. I asked her what kind of sailing experience she and Todd had. Todd had not had any, and Renee's experience was with her dad on a Sunfish on a lake when she was young, so this was quite an undertaking for them—really for anyone. I was glad we were with them. I myself almost had an anxiety attack one afternoon when I realized where we were—a speck in the middle of the ocean with nobody else there. I really had to grab a hold of my mind, or I would have lost it. As a result, I have gained compassion for those who suffer from panic and anxiety.

Janet and I also stood watch together at night. We would hide under the table from the wind and the pelting rain. This reminded me of the story in the Bible when all the disciples were sailing in a storm—the NIV says, "Jesus was sleeping on the cushion." The disciples were disturbed by this, but our comfort sprang out of that verse as Janet and I would point to the cushion nearby. We knew Jesus was just sleeping, and we could wake him up if we needed him. That's what got me across the Pacific on one of the roughest crossings I have ever experienced. Twenty days of constant on-the-nose wind. We were called "the wrong-way sailors." We found out later that a submarine off the coast of Hawaii was actually watching us through their periscope. Reportedly, only about six boats come that way a year.

We arrived in Kauai in August 2008. The dock looked very threatening; stepping onto land after a lengthy voyage, people often experience land sickness. After twenty days of rough seas, I was a bit nervous about how severe the dizziness might possibly be. Walking is the best way to overcome it, and for sure, we had to stay out of small enclosed places!

I have to say that Renee was a trooper. She was experiencing migraines on this crossing but never once complained. It was a bonding journey—one I believe none of us will forget. Renee and I ended up flying from Hawaii back to the mainland of California. I bought a truck after getting off the redeye flight into LA and drove to Washington State.

While waiting for my family to return, I spent time with friends windsurfing on the Columbia River Gorge. Ted, Trevor, Todd, and Janet continued to sail the last leg to San Diego, California. The weather conditions did not improve but worsened. They spent seventeen days in rough seas with the wind peaking at forty knots, relentlessly pounding *Gabriella*. The ambient water temperature cooled the boat down into a floating refrigerator. Since we had been in the tropics the entire time, cold weather clothing was nil. The trampoline nets on *Gabriella* were blown out by the seas. Water filled the front lockers, the pounding seas detached the dining table in the main salon, and the waves took half our gear off the deck.

One morning, Todd woke Ted and said, "I think there is something wrong with the boat."

Ted got up to a waterfall of saltwater inside the boat coming from the cockpit through the main salon and into the hulls. The waves were crashing over the boat. My son was only sixteen years old at this time, enduring a time at sea that you don't want to repeat, but that hasn't scared my son off because today he is a merchant mariner and loves the sea. After they finally made it to port, I drove down the west coast of the United States and was happy to be rejoined with the "wrong-way sailors" in San Diego!

I questioned my time aboard *Gabriella*, wondering what it was all about. What I had envisioned for the voyage was different from the reality I experienced, but I would not trade my experience for anything in the world. I had a great time with my family. We bonded as a team with no regrets! My eyes also have been opened to the reality of others, and I was taken out of my safe bubble in the United States. I saw people cooking over fires with dirt floors; houses made of reed in the wilderness and houses made of debris in the city; clothing which represented tribes, culture, and displayed meaning; men in skirts and countless girls having babies in puberty; kayaks made of wood; taking on water; sailing the sea with only coconuts for food. Mainly I saw many people living in what an American would call lack. I was very attracted to them. I found them to be happy and joyful, exuding a freedom from their souls which I lacked. I felt embraced, welcomed, and accepted. They would love to practice speaking English, and I would relish that time to learn some Spanish.

Before departing *Gabriella*, Renee and I were reflecting and taking on the question "What do you want in your life now?" We both were headed into a time of transition. It occurred to me that I wanted certainty, and I wanted to be part of a team because what we can do together is greater than what one can do alone. I also asked God what this sailing trip was all about. In my mind, I heard him answer, "I will love you unconditionally forever." God has given back to me more than a hundredfold of what the devil had stolen from me. He is the giver of life; my faith and trust is in him. Life is not about race, and it is not about color. Whether we are American, Guatemalan, Q'eqchi, or anyone else in the world, this is the only certainly we have: God loves us unconditionally forever.

With all the miles and everything in between, Guatemala keeps calling me. Something very special was lodged in my heart. I remember the tears when we departed the river on our sailing adventure many years ago. God has a plan, and he prepares us for his plan. Here I am today after many twists and turns. Wave after wave, he continues to reveal his great and mysterious ways.

GAIL GORDON

Gail, Ted and baby gg

3

Nine Women in the Jungle

After returning to America from our sailing adventure, my life in the Florida Keys was a time of transition. At first, I was excited about what was ahead even though I did not know what it was. My excitement soon turned to darkness. I was having difficulty relating to my friends. Common conversations were about your children and your home—the most basic things in life—but I was not able to connect. Life had radically changed for me, and my focus had been altered. The heartache of the world was screaming in my ear along with my own personal life shifting so drastically.

The economy of America was collapsing at an alarming rate. The boom of the housing market crashed, foreclosures were happening at an alarming rate, and many in the business world were going bankrupt. The spirit of depression was in the air, and it was contagious. At the same time, my father-in-law, Bill, was dying, which weighed me down even more. As my husband cared for him, it was one of the most difficult seasons of our lives, but it grew into one of the most rewarding times. After a year's time and a series of blood clots, Bill passed away in the VA Hospital in Miami. To watch a person you love who has always been so vibrant fading away and struggling on multiple levels brings a great sense of loss and powerlessness. My father-in-law had lost his leg in a dive accident many years prior, but it did not slow him down. His motto was "Yes you can!" long before President Obama made the saying popular. He was close to seventy years of age when he founded Admiral Handicapped Scuba Adventures, a nonprofit organization founded to teach handicapped people to dive and find freedom in the water. This organization became the root of Blue Water Surrender.

Prior to his passing away, I started helping Bill with his organization. His health was declining, and at the same time, my husband and I were thinking about establishing our own official nonprofit. Even though our mission ahead had not yet been revealed, yet somehow a seed was germinating. God is timeless and moves between dimensions. He knows even when we do not. Bill decided to pass his nonprofit over to us. On August 20, 2009, we changed the name and the mission. Admiral Handicapped Scuba Adventures became Blue Water Surrender.

My father-in-law, Bill, loved children. He was a baby magnet! If there was a baby in the room, it was only seconds until the baby was in his arms, and Bill's face would have the biggest smile, lit up with joy. During the same season, our family dog Ayla passed away in my arms. I had asked God for compassion, to take her life quickly, and I heard in my mind, "I am putting compassion in your hands." Compassion did not come without great pain. My son was already settled in at Maine Maritime Academy when Ayla died, and my empty nest was becoming even more empty. The vacancy in my heart was expanding. It is wonderful to see your child grow and go off into the world, especially in such a good direction, but the pain I experienced when dropping him off was one I was not prepared for. Ayla was the last of the familiar personalities in my life to pass away at that time. Everything had changed since returning from sailing. More of what I loved had been stripped away. Open hands, open heart, but tears in my eyes. My joy was fading. As I looked around, all I saw was an empty house. Would I ever fill it again?

I would wake up at night, sorrowful, and walk out to the water, pining for the rocking of our boat *Gabriella*. I would remember all the people I met and the places I was so blessed to see. In church I would start crying for Guatemala for no reason at all—it would just hit me. I was not able to hold back the pain I felt; I had to release it in tears. I now believe tears are our best prayers, and your mission chooses you.

In this extremely difficult season of my life, God was faithful to build beauty from ashes. One profound evidence of God's hand and plan in preparing me as a missionary came through my father-in-law as he passed on his nonprofit status to us. There are many things in life we do not understand in the moment. As time passes and we look back, we often see the tapestry that was being woven.

I had seen Bill's heart draw close to God over the years. I saw clearly how he loved children and how he loved Guatemala as he took many trips in his later years to study Spanish in Antigua. After he passed away, we were on a boating mission trip to Guatemala, and we brought his prosthetic leg in the hope that someone there might benefit from it. When we arrived and were unloading an overwhelming amount of medical supplies, a US doctor and his wife came to ask if we needed help. The doctor just happened to be a prosthetic expert! We asked him about Bill's leg, and he said it would be very hard to find a match for it, but the one true God of the universe connected us through Luis to the Range of Motion Project (ROMP), where they refurbish prosthetics. It was a heartfelt moment when I met Martha, the lady who had lost her leg from being hit by a car. To see her walk with Bill's prosthesis and have a new life is a glimpse into God's amazing heart! The fact that we got to meet her in person and see this miracle for ourselves was overwhelming. God has a heart to show himself to us to demonstrate that what we do and think and pray matters. He will answer our prayers.

Since that time, I have personally met many Americans and Guatemalans who are active in ROMP. There is such a great feeling of being part of God's family, working together for his purposes. Even though what we each do is uniquely different from what anyone else does, he puts it all together as one beautiful picture of his grace and mercy working through a united body. There is nothing like it!

The lesson I had already learned by that time is that life is a series of "letting go," and it now reached me on a much deeper level. All the events in our lives prepare us for something greater, and that was true for me as well. The valley of darkness, with its cloud of tears, fought with me for years. I would come up for air and then get pushed back down. I wondered if I would ever walk all the way through it, but there is water and light in the desert—it is not just a mirage on the horizon. God loves us so much—he doesn't leave us in the valley. Throughout these times of trial, the Lord was working on my heart and my mind to set me free from things that were hindering my walk. The more we are able to let go of the very obstacles that God is working to remove, the more of God we will experience.

In this season of my life, I was searching for something new or something more in my life. With all the free time I now had and no responsibilities to speak of, I was inspired to return to Guatemala especially after a few conversations about the Rio Dulce area of Guatemala with my friends Anna and Butch. They are ocean-loving Florida Keys people who had been contemplating repairs to their sailboat. The beautiful Rio Dulce was becoming very inviting to me especially adding the thought of a mission trip into the mix.

The day came when we loaded their beautiful Bristol 54 with medical supplies and sailed like a rocket through the winds and waves to the Rio Dulce. My heart was thrilled to reconnect with the area and people I had met. On that trip, I was able to witness the presence of God and how he makes a way and places people in your path to guide and direct you. Missions were grabbing ahold of my heart. This trip led to another trip by air which was just as wonderful. Every time I landed back in America, my heart would dream of heading back out. One day, out of the blue, Luis called me from Guatemala. I wasn't aware of it yet, but he was being used by God as a catalyst for change in my life. Little did I know at this time what a great tree would grow, new from the seed of this phone call.

My interest in mission trips to Guatemala was becoming contagious. Each trip led to the next; a breadcrumb trail from heaven was falling. At times I was reluctant and somewhat afraid. This was new, but faith and curiosity continued to lead the way. I started traveling to Guatemala more often and inviting everyone who came across my path. Flights were very reasonable, and the US dollar was going very far. God was growing me up for his purpose; a passionate fire to experience more of God was burning in my heart to share with others.

A TRAIL OF THE HOLY SPIRIT

Astonishingly, we encountered great success from the beginning. We spent time at churches focusing on the children, and it had a great impact. Our teams would create skits, games, and activities to share with the many excited children. It would not be uncommon to have more than a hundred children at a gathering where we were expecting twenty—we learned very quickly how to improvise. Some of my fondest memories are during our children's ministry outreaches with our teams, comprised mainly of friends from the Florida Keys. As time progressed, people would join us from other cities and states and, eventually, from other countries.

Each trip would lay the foundation for the next. Once while out walking in the small village of Esmeralda, I met a pastor carrying a large part of a tree. I asked him what he was doing, and he said he was building a children's church and showed me his work so far. Being relatively new in Guatemala, I was astounded by the sight of a donkey wandering around, and I certainly did not understand rough lumber freshly cut from trees. This was a whole new world where people cooked over fire and swept dirt floors. The pastor spoke about a village up in the mountains called Rio Frio and a girls' camp in the Petén region. Well, you know I had to go, but there was not time for both. Rio Frio was closer, so the girls' camp would have to wait for a later date.

We hired a couple of rugged trucks which would withstand the terrain and the winding dirt roads which passed through a good-sized river without a bridge plus a stream or two. I was intrigued with such rough wilderness and beauty as we passed under the tall trees that gave us shade. The trek there was filled with the most wonderful sounds of exotic birds and tree frogs singing out. The air currents in the jungle were nothing like I had experienced before. The jungle itself seemed to be breathing in and out in the heavy, fragrant air. We ended up hiking up into the mountains to the village after passing through a river in our truck then getting stuck in the mud. Our cell phone still worked, so we were able to call for help. Men from the village came down and helped us carry our supplies. We hiked the rest of the way through the jungle, leaving our truck temporarily stuck in the steep muddy mountainside. The sounds were thrilling, and the tall trees were mysterious to me; I fell in love with the beauty that surrounded me.

We continued sailing down from Florida to Guatemala in boats loaded with medical supplies and school supplies for the children. There is never a shortage of need at home or abroad. I believe it is important to listen to what is calling your heart. Each person has something within them that drives them beyond their own personal strength. This is what I consider the call of God on our lives. Answering that call is the greatest life one can lead, and where it will go has endless possibilities.

As I said before, the suffering in the world has taught me compassion and still compels me, even so many years later, to alleviate that suffering. Compared to the rest of the world, America dwells in an extremely fortunate culture, but many of us are not even aware of this. I personally never realized it before I set sail even with my own encounters with poverty. Just being born in the United States, you have many freedoms others do not have. We are able to travel in and out of our country in great freedom to many other countries—at least prior to COVID. This is not necessarily so for others from different countries. We may take the ability to read and write for granted, along with many other blessings, but our country is ready to lend a hand of help when tragedy hits around the globe. We are not perfect, but I believe the core of America has good intentions. In the US, many programs provide for those in need. Assistance with food, medical care, and education is available. On the contrary, in Guatemala, medically needy people walk for miles to arrive at volunteer clinics; it is the only hope they may have. Many are waiting for medical mission teams to come so that they can receive treatment and surgery which are unavailable otherwise. Others will get on their knees and pray, keeping hope in the healing power of God. In the public hospital of Guatemala, medicine is often not available, and you will need an advocate to care for you during your stay. In many public hospitals, there is no chair for that person to sit on, and they will spend the night under the hospital bed of the patient. For many people, just getting to the hospital is a hardship. To come up with the money to take the bus while suffering with a serious illness—never mind having money for food to eat—looks impossible for many. The entire population of Guatemala is not in this position; there are wealthy Guatemalans—many who are able to care for their families and care for them well—but what I am describing does stand true for a large portion of the people.

Other norms in the US differ from the norms in Guatemala too. In America, we take our children out for chicken fingers and French fries. In rural Guatemala, a child may be out in back of the house plucking the feathers off the fresh-killed chicken which had been running around the house and yard for the last few months, treated like a pet. Education differs greatly between the two countries: the average educational level of children in rural areas is the sixth grade while most American children finish grade twelve. Higher grades are offered in Guatemala, but only a small percentage continue for various reasons, often financial. The deeper you go into the jungle or the mountains, the less education you will find. I do not see many rural children riding bicycles with super-cool helmets on. What I see are toys made of old pieces of wood, plastic bottles, and caps. The rural people are excellent at recycling and recreating with wonderful smiles! Additionally, a Guatemalan child's life isn't all about fun and games. Children work, helping their parents. Young girls carry bowls of corn on their heads to be ground at the *molina*. They will use the ground corn paste to make tortillas. Looking out to a lake or river, it is not uncommon to see girls and women doing laundry. Young boys will work in the field. They will carry a machete and become adept at using it at a very young age. I have seen a four-year-old child carrying a machete, and he knew how to use it. Both young boys and girls may be sent to town to sell products made at home or produce from the field. In our American streets, we often see dogs and cats. In the villages, pigs, chickens and geese wander about. Food is cooked over wood fires, and floors are often compressed dirt. A turtle may be tied up on a string for dinner because there is no refrigeration. These are just some of the common differences, and there are many more. What I notice most in all of this—the children and adults smile from an inner joy, and this is very compelling!

I don't believe in renovating someone else's culture. I find each culture unique with its own beautiful way of life. However, I do feel it is important to help those who are suffering within different cultures to help bring healing to the body, the mind, and the soul. To those who are willing to receive what you have to offer in Jesus's name, you must be mindful to help and not hurt. It is important to think our actions through. "What will help?" is a very important question to ask yourself before you start doing anything.

Kingdom life is a process of learning; with every action taken, we learn more; and we are not alone in our efforts—we are able to learn from others who have been called to help. It is important to look at the intention of your heart; is it entirely pure? Or is there a hidden agenda? Check your motive: is it unconditional love? You must never think of yourself as being superior to another because that would be placing yourself in God's position. We are all on this planet together; we are one human race with different gifts and talents. No one is above anyone else, especially in God's eyes, so no one is to think more highly of oneself than others (Romans 12:3). We are called to make disciples in all nations (Matthew 28:18–20).

Our minds are powerful. You live what you are learning, as life loves to teach. The question is are you willing to learn? As a missionary, a messenger, the culture you happen to be walking into is more than a country. Your thoughts and your feelings, how you operate is the force within that is driving you. It's good to pay attention to our motives and goals as we often live on autopilot and miss out on so much. Awareness is a gift that brings life as we choose well. Scripture tells us to practice agape love, to put others first, and nowhere is that more important than in ministry. Love is way more than a feeling. It is a mindset, a stance, a safeguard against damaging the people you are trying to help. Only God can change a person or a culture. It's important to leave that job in his hands while you demonstrate his love.

Continuing this thinking on agape love, I have to say that I love mission trips! They are opportunities to join with others, make new friends, and come alongside people as colaborers. One of my greatest examples of colaboring is my ministry friend Luis. One of his tasks was to drive our teams to many faraway places; most of the time we were somewhere in Guatemala and at times somewhere in Honduras. Each day, as we headed out as a team, I liked to have an intention for the day, a godly trait to focus on such as love, mercy, or grace and be very intentional about it. What you learn as you focus on a certain quality will emerge organically without struggling for it. Agape love should flow freely the way Jesus ministered, so it's important to develop it like a muscle.

One trip changed the course of our mission to this region. I was starting to think about all the need and pain in the world and began to contemplate what is most important. Where is the greatest pain? What would I so desperately want help for? Physical pain without hope is on the top of my list. I have experienced that myself in my life, but thanks to a dear friend of mine, Katie, I am alive today.

I had gone to the emergency room and was diagnosed with an ovarian cyst. After being declined for treatment by my insurance and having no money or credit card to use, I was sent home, and I became even sicker. Katie came to help me, driving me to doctor after doctor until a generous and kind doctor rushed me to the hospital for emergency surgery, so I know what it means to suffer physically without a remedy, but I also know what it's like to finally be delivered from that condition. Ministering to people who are suffering is lifesaving and life giving.

Next on my list is food—feeding the hungry. Have you ever gone without food for a long time? It is painful, and when you have no money to buy food and no job to make money, life seems hopeless. If you doubt this, I can assure you that it is so. I have lived this while I was young due to my own poor decisions. Hunger is debilitating on many levels. It causes disease and makes it hard to think and learn. This brings us to education: it is a gift, and it is extremely important to be able to go to school to learn a new way of life so when a child grows up, he or she will be able to have a job, obtain food, and feed a family. These are all earthly needs which need cultivation, but we must think deeper, past merely life on earth. As Scripture teaches, our human lives are like a breath, and our lifespans are like shadows (Psalm 144:4). The Word of God is eternal, and without the word of truth, we will perish for eternity, so food and other earthly needs, as important as they are, become secondary. Although each need is connected to one another, you can see how it is difficult to keep a focus on just one need. I see why missions expand into building homes, creating schools, equipping hospitals, planting churches, and sustaining feeding programs. In many ways, my mission life has touched all five of these crucial areas.

Do you ever feel overwhelmed by the suffering in the world? Take heart! God will guide us all in our calling, and the most important mission is the one placed in front of you in the moment you are in. I was in such a moment in a village I frequented and loved. While in the small village church, the pastor shared with me about a girl's camp up in the mountains where young girls lived with their babies. This caught my attention—"What do you mean, 'young girls and babies'?" I asked. Another lesson of harsh reality was ahead.

Why did I begin to focus on the needs of children? Children are the next generation and will bring forth the future—either good or bad. Jesus loves the little children. We are not to hinder them. They are to be loved and cared for (Matthew 19:14). You can never go wrong to empower children in truth, to build them up in love and supply their basic needs. The seeds we plant today have an effect on the tomorrows to come. Weeds that have been planted from the past need to be removed with gentleness and care. New seeds of love, spoken and demonstrated, can change the direction in which they will grow. Moreover, God promised to bless the children of his faithful ones as well as their children's children (Genesis 17:7; Deuteronomy 6:6–7). When we nurture children, we nurture the future.

Why is it necessary for us to go into the world to reach out to people for Christ? Can't God do the reaching for us? Yes, but he blesses us by allowing us to be his hands and feet. He created us for good works which he prepared for each of us ahead of time (Ephesians 2:10). God is always preparing our hearts for what is next. Just take a look at your life and see how the pieces start to fit together and are interwoven, creating something new within and around your being. All that we experience in life is used for good when we are walking in the kingdom of God; nothing is wasted. The word says we transition from glory to glory; well, it doesn't always feel glorious, but glorious it shall be. This is the way God makes things unfold through our hands and our hearts. I know with absolute certainty that God has shaped me into a catalyst for redemption. He is no respecter of persons; this is his calling in his kingdom.

This is where nine women in the jungle comes in—a mission trip that set the course for what one day would lead to Casa Agua Azul. A door was in the process of being opened. In November 2012, I was leading the nine women, not knowing what lay ahead. Our brave but fun-loving team consisted of Carolyn, Christi, Mary, Joanne, Liza, Irevi, Tracey, Chris, and myself. The women were excited, and as good women and moms, we had over two thousand pounds of luggage on our American Airlines flight filled with gifts for the children! We were headed to a children's home of a wonderful missionary couple I had met while sailing with my family.

The flight landed in San Pedro Sula, Honduras, where Luis and our driver, Otilio, picked us up. I am not so sure they had experienced this much luggage before, but good Guatemalan men that they are, they managed to tie it all down on the roof of our van and the back of the pickup truck. Happily, with a cup of good Honduran coffee in hand, we were eventually on our way, driving though Honduras into Guatemala.

A funny thing had happened. We had planned on and were prepared to stay and minister at a children's home in the Rio Dulce region, a visit which had been previously arranged, but sometimes God has other plans. At the last minute, without notice, something had come up, and the plans to stay at the home were canceled. Luis, resourceful person that he is, found a house on a tributary tucked away off the beaten path. The owner was a doctor from Guatemala City, and she was overjoyed to have us as guests. What a delight! We called our new place "The Tree House." You have to take a boat to get to this house, and with all that luggage, Luis and Otilio had some more fun ahead! It was perfect, and we all fell in love with the quaint, artistic house built from beautiful local hardwoods. We found ourselves immersed in the sounds of the jungle, which was making beautiful music to our ears. Those ever-present exotic birds echoing through the branches along with the tree frogs make the most beautiful ever-changing symphony.

Our group had some organizing and sorting of goods ahead from our many suitcases. We also had no mission plan now. As I said before, things don't always go as planned in missions. Back to the drawing board to discover what God had in mind. As the leader, this places a little pressure on my entire being especially when some of these women had never been on an overseas mission in a land way different than their own. However, everyone's enthusiasm never went away.

Carolyn divided us into two teams with team names—the Joyfuls and the Faithfuls. This added to the fun. They were all eager to serve and were ready for whatever was ahead. After we had finished sorting out all our luggage supplies, there was a lull in time. As we were discussing what to do next, time seemed to stop, and we all looked at each other, dazed. Large waves were lapping on the dock. Being from the Florida Keys, I thought a big boat had gone by, leaving a wake—but wait. We were on a small tributary; only small boats could get up this creek.

We had just experienced our first earthquake in Guatemala. It was a very strange sensation. What followed next was the announcement on the news that Barack Obama had been elected president of the United States. More surprises were ahead.

The first few days of any trip typically bring confusion. After years of leading mission trips, I have found this mild chaos to be normal. Many questions, along with heightened emotions, arise while adjusting to a new culture and routine. I know now to expect these things to precede the harmony which comes as all find their place and begin to function as a unified team, which is beautiful to witness. God is faithful to bring things together. People come excited, ready to serve, but often they will find that God is already in motion, doing a mighty work on their own heart first. The refining fire is always present—no one is exempt. I have learned so much and grown considerably in my faith on the mission field. When you think you have surrendered, you will find there is more to surrender.

A TRAIL OF THE HOLY SPIRIT

Throughout our time in Guatemala, the Spirit of God was moving constantly, touching our hearts. God spoke to each of us in many ways through his written word, situations, dreams, words that others spoke, and in our minds in visions. These pictures and words led us to experience profound moments of encounter as we worked together. God reveals and confirms his truth in bits and pieces, and there are sudden moments where it will come together and exhilarate your soul to no end. This trip was no exception—it was exceptional! Sometimes what is heard and seen in your spirit is vague, and you are unable to put into words what is happening, but you know deep inside something is being birthed. When a child is conceived, you begin to sense that, but it is months later that you see the evidence and are able to find out the sex of the child, and so it often is with our spirits. This is what I saw—that new seeds were being planted, and new life would be birthed. Each one received something different, unique, as the Holy Spirit's fire was lit and starting to burn.

After waking in the tree house every morning, the team would pile into a small riverboat to make our way across the water to the town dock. One of the ladies, whom we nicknamed Moo, just had a heart procedure two days before the trip. Her doctor released her, and she came on the trip! I thought she was rather crazy or filled with massive faith to come on a rustic trip so soon. It was not so easy for her to get in or out of the boat, but with a determined team, we had success every day.

One of our very talented team members had prepared a skit to witness the love of God to the children, and we all were in need of learning the skit! Unfortunately, something kept interfering with this. Frustration was building for good reason as I was not able to keep my word to her that we would take time to practice. One morning, as we were headed into town, I felt I would never be out of the doghouse if we did not stop and give my blessed friend our time. Reaching the dinghy dock, we all climbed out of the boat under the bridge that towers eighty feet over the Rio Dulce (which means "sweet river" in Spanish). At the bridge, the river separates two land masses, forming a main throughway of the country.

As we all took our positions and listened to the instructions for performing the skit, I turned my head, astonished. I yelled, "Stop! Stop!" as they all looked at me with great wonder. Next, I said, "Take a picture!" No one else could comprehend my great moment in time. I was astounded as I found myself standing in the middle of a mysterious dream which I had months prior. In my dream I was standing in that exact spot, looking up from under the bridge across the waterway and seeing dirty water, native people, and feeling extremely sad. My heart was deeply impacted even though it did not make sense to me, but most dreams usually don't. Nothing earth-shattering happened in this moment except what took place inside me. God had shown me this moment of time through a dream. Although I had never stood there before, this moment of recognition affirmed in my heart that I was in the right place, walking according to God's plan, and that God does speak to people.

In the days to come, more light was shed on my dream as I experienced the different parts of the dream. Often dreams become revelations which hold a still deeper meaning to be discerned in the days to come. There were three parts to the dream; this moment was only the first part. The second part came when another member's grandfather died while she was on the trip. The great sadness in the dream revealed itself then. The third part was when I returned home. After having my special moment, we continued practicing the skit, and later in the day, we had so much fun sharing it with others.

In that place and time, words of prophecy were spoken over many team members by three pastors who came across our path as well as Luis's wife, Heidi, all given with profound meaning to each person who received them. For myself, three different prophecies were spoken at three different times. I had never experienced this before in my life. I had a hard time believing what was happening to me as it was blowing my mind. I kept seeing things being born in the Spirit throughout the trip. This was all new and rather surreal. I almost felt like I was back in high school and someone had slipped me a bit of LSD, causing me to hallucinate the entire trip. In spite of the dreamlike character of my experiences, God was becoming more real than ever!

A TRAIL OF THE HOLY SPIRIT

Later on in our mission's journey, we arrived at a tiny church tucked away in the village of Saila. People were starting to gather, but suddenly I was called outside, leaving everything in my dear friend Christi's hands. God showed me that I could trust her with anything; when I walked back in, a party was going on, and the whole church was worshiping, filled with joy! I was glad that Christi had led the people into rejoicing and worship, but while I was outside, what I had experienced was nothing like ever before. The pastor started prophesying to me, telling me things about my life which no one knew, bringing tears to my eyes and healing to my heart. He had imparted something to me that manifested very quickly within the same hour.

Mary, one of the team members, was outside at the same time. She was a girl from Michigan, a friend of Christi's, who had decided to join the team. She was not feeling well and was standing with Moo, our prayer warrior. I went over to them and placed my hand on Mary's belly. It felt as if she was pregnant and giving birth in the Spirit, and that moment of time is when this ministry of Blue Water Surrender was born. This may sound strange to you, and I will say in a sense it is; but as you continue to walk with God, this is life with Holy Spirit, the third person of the Trinity. God reveals his plans to us through his Spirit. He will tell us things that we had no way of knowing (Jeremiah 33:3), and he will often confirm his message in unexpected ways.

When we returned to the house that night, I was stunned again. The cleaning lady had gone above and beyond her normal duties and folded the towels into sailboats! This touched my heart deeply! She also laid a necklace of purple beads along with my sword on my bed. The purple beads and sword, a plastic one for skits, had a personal meaning behind it. The beads represent royalty to me, and the sword was authority. There was a sailboat there also and a mola. Again, God was encouraging me to step forward, assuring me that he was with me, emboldening me to take my place which he has prepared for me in advance.

I was still reluctant to accept and embrace who I am in Christ. We all have resurrection power within, and to come into that truth can be a profound awakening. Still I was having trouble believing—then a third prophecy came. In this prophecy, I was being called "a mother to many" and was seeing the ministry being poured forth. God is so faithful and patient with us. He is not going to hit us over the head with a two-by-four. He will pour his tremendous love over your heart over and over again. The common denominator with all the words spoken over my life was "mother to many." I did not know what it meant, and I was not sure I liked it. "Mother to many" means I was not a kid anymore! *Time to grow up!*

Our journey into the jungle region of Guatemala continued to the girl's camp I had heard about from the pastor in the village church of Esmeralda. We arrived after a long drive of nearly three hours, packed into Otilio's van like happy sardines. The camp turned out to be a children's home to twenty-one abandoned, abused, precious children. The dwelling space was in need of some help, but it was a loving home. A Guatemalan couple ran the house—Papa Beto and Mama Coney. Their hearts were filled with love for the children, and our group fell in heartbroken love for them all!

Mama Coney was determined to build a proper house for the children nearby. She had big plans and big faith in a mighty God and broke ground with a hoe and a child on her hip. A man next door at the restaurant saw her and went over to her, asking what she was doing. She told him she was going to build a home for the children! This man, touched by her determination and compassion, supplied building materials to get started on construction. Up to that point, Mama Coney had accomplished the purchase of the land. The hoe in the ground was the start of the construction. It is astonishing what one person can do while stepping out in faith, with God in your heart and at your side.

Next, Mama Coney shared with me that a woman from the Rio Dulce area mysteriously found her way out to the construction site and supplied more funds for building materials; and just then, I stood praying with them, looking at a partial foundation, knowing the money had run out and back wages needed to be paid to move forward. My heart sank, gazing at her deferred hope. As we drove back to the Rio, there was not a dry eye in the van. Most of us were mothers, and the thought of these children's plight was too much for our hearts to bear.

Christi, filled with compassion, decided to take a step of faith and host a dinner back home in the states to pay the back debt so they would be able to move forward. I felt encouraged that my heart was not the only one moved to take action.

As we spent much time in prayer during that mission trip, our sense of the anointed presence of God increased more and more. We had the opportunity to stop and visit the other children's home, the one we originally planned on visiting. This home was beautiful, and they raised the children as a family, taking only twelve in at a time. We had a wonderful day learning more about Guatemala and her culture. Our skit finally came to life, blessing the hearts of all present with the theme of "Lead me to the cross, where transformation takes place."

God loves us through the little things in life. Nothing goes unnoticed with the Lord. Being there with people, for people really matters. For instance, a small bolt of white fabric, which Christi felt she had to bring, not knowing why, became an answered prayer to the mother of the house. This house mother teaches the girls sewing and crafts. She had been praying for the white fabric for one of their projects. More tears flowed as God touched hearts in these small but meaningful gestures of love. Love never fails. When you feel that feeling within yourself, go with it in faith and watch. See yourself in a God encounter that will be so special and intimate to your heart. You will crave this more and more.

This journey of nine women in the jungle changed many lives of those who journeyed, bringing a renewed fire home to our communities. New ministries came into being, and our faith was built stronger along with our bond together. What we experienced in concert is tied between our hearts, beyond what words can say. Short-term mission trips avail much. Fire has been placed in our hands, and it is faith that will keep it alive.

We returned home to the Florida Keys with a full heart. As Christmas neared, I received a call. It was Luis from Guatemala again. He shared with me there had been a fire—a terrible fire. Casa Achiam was destroyed, and Momma Coney was in great distress. They were all blessed to be alive, but everything was torched to the ground—not even a shoe left behind. Now the children were homeless, taking refuge in a church and sleeping on the floor. It was fortunate no lives were lost, but everything inside the house was destroyed. It is hard to do nothing about a situation when the names and faces of lives you have touched are involved. We had to do something immediately.

In order to take quick action, we decided to have a yard sale to raise funds to help build the new building. I had never wanted to raise money for a building, but I now saw the value of this effort. It is not the building itself; it is what takes place within. It is a roof that protects and walls that shelter. As we place a roof over the children's heads, their hearts have a chance to heal. This yard sale was huge! Items came in by the truckload and never seemed to stop. The day of the sale, as items went out and as neighbors learned the purpose of our sale, they started bringing more items to the sale. It was incredible and profitable. God was moving on behalf of the children. We were able to help, and my faith was increasing.

I am one of the last people on earth who wants to ask for money, yet I was starting to become one of the first despite my major discomfort. Blue Water Surrender was coming into fruition to bless the children. I saw God moving, and it was planted in my heart to be a part of getting this building done. We became a Florida 501(c)(3) to be able to take in the donations.

The core group of Blue Water Surrender consisted of our small Bible study group combined with the nine women in the jungle. One day, as we were studying one of those step-out-in-faith-and-follow-the-Spirit-of-God books, we ladies challenged each other. I heard them say words to the effect of "You need to do a fundraiser." Ugh, my unfavorite word—officially asking many people for money. Oh no, this is way outside of my comfort zone. Besides I was sailing to the Bahamas soon to work with the Boy Scouts of America doing sailing adventures. How would I do both?

God is always our answer even when the question seems too big. He works through faith, unity, and people. At our next Bible study meeting, I announced my answer to the challenge. I said "Okay, I will step out of my box. Let's do a fundraiser." They were all excited, ready, and happy to pitch in. I continued, "We will have a fish fry. I know a place. I will ask Richard at Bud 'n' Mary's Marina to have it there, but I am going to the Bahamas soon." Somehow, we pulled it off in a couple of months and raised $16,000, not having a clue about what we were doing.

I am in a fortunate position because of my husband's support and the blessings of God. I am free to travel and am able to dedicate my life to this mission. Being the steward of funds placed in my hands, with faith, for a purpose, I began traveling to Guatemala on a regular basis. Support kept coming in. In 2014, our organization's efforts, along with many others including the Church of God, who is the steward of the house, completed the home for those twenty-one children who had captured our hearts.

Those twenty-one grew in number, eventually reaching fifty-six in no time at all. I was visiting often, and it was evident that the physical, emotional, and spiritual needs of the children were great and ongoing on every level. The joy of succeeding in our efforts was tempered by the plight faced by so many of the children in that region. The deprivation was apparent; one house could only hold so many children.

Luis, my mission partner, and his wife, Heidi, saw this too, and they started to talk about the need for another home. A big seed was being planted in their hearts. Luis had a dream and said to me, "One day, you will have a house on the water where you will come in a sailboat and have many children." I was not so certain I believed this, but I suspected this was another confirmation of the "mother to many" prophecy again. God was turning on another light, sculpting beauty from ashes in multiple forms. A new stream of living water was about to spring forth.

GAIL GORDON

The dream under the bridge

4

The House by the Water

Miracles have happened and continue to happen. Fought-for faith, often with great resistance, has been my battle—to believe the blessing of the Lord is here after years of waiting. King Solomon spent seven years building the house of God in Jerusalem (1 Kings 9:10-11).

In comparison, I spent seven years building Casa Agua Azul, God's house for the children.

Many times, I prayed for things that I would consider a miracle. My troubles were often more than double. Despite the challenges on the mission field, God always led the way. Sometimes you just have to look a little harder, listen a little deeper, and always wait. While the Coronavirus continued to breathe down our necks, Scripture teaches us that we are to thank God in all circumstances for everything. God knows why I am here. I am certain he has a plan. Governments all around the world assessed the pandemic and protected what is loved and irreplaceable—their people. Borders were shutting down not just in Guatemala but around the world. Panic was not the only thing in the air. In the spirit, I was seeing a love so great that I was overwhelmed. God's presence was powerful and speaking to my heart. Each day the puzzle pieces started to fit together. Instead of asking myself why I was here, I started looking to see how I could be of service.

In this crazy time, I was meeting baby Gail Nahomy for the first time, and it was difficult to see her terribly ill. To top it off, there was no running water in the house. No water was a big problem. Our water pump refused to work any longer. I walked onto the scene of the women and girls washing sheets and mosquito nets in the lake. Blanca, after being up until 2:30 a.m., was among them, and it was early in the morning. Our nannies were getting exhausted and fearful of the unknown at this point. We needed help quickly. Handwashing was crucial and would be difficult along with carrying buckets from the lake to flush the toilets.

Under normal circumstances, my concern would be rather small, considering the situation was just another day in Guatemala; but with the onset of Coronavirus, we needed a solution without any delay. A new water pump from the hardware store was necessary, and we had received word it was closing at 5:00 p.m. and would not reopen for another twenty-one days; we needed clean running water to keep everyone healthy. With midday approaching, I considered this an emergency.

Facebook came in handy to raise the needed extra funds. By sending a message saying "*Ayudame!*" which means "I need help!" in Spanish, miraculous provision immediately came in within an hour. Jerry and I jumped in the car, rushing to town forty-five minutes away. By 3:30 in the afternoon, we were out of the hardware store with the most prized possession—a 1.5 horsepower water pump and a few miscellaneous parts. People were in chaos, and to find a plumber and an electrician by sunset would take a miracle. Thank God, help arrived, and the electricity was working on this day—it has a habit of going out, sometimes for days. As our story continues, we didn't meet our deadline of sunset, but flashlights are a great invention. At 8:30 p.m. we heard the sweet sound of running water. Clean water means life.

When we first started renovating the house in 2015, running water was a big issue. For some reason, the village would not allow us to hook up to the water system. This is a double miracle because when I look back, I prayed for the money to build the cistern and purchase our first water pump. A special donor simply wrote a check for the children and said, "It's done," and God continues to supply miraculously. This wonderful angel of a woman was the one who answered the call again. We are extremely grateful for her big heart for the children.

As I look back in time, the renovation of the house was a huge undertaking. Before you decide to renovate a house, you need to own the house and the property it rests on. This requires a lot of money, so be certain you buy the right house! How do you know it is the right house? My answer is research! This may take some time and, in our case, some extensive travel. You can't always trust just yourself. That's what friends are for!

Bert and Jeff are just that—good friends and have been by my side from the beginning. Back in 2014, When I became serious about purchasing the house for a children's home, they joined Ted and me on a sailing journey. We sailed from Florida aboard our second catamaran, *Adonai*, to do a reconnaissance trip. It was a five-day sail to Guatemala. At one point, I felt as if I had dragged them all into the jungle of Guatemala; in my mind, it was halfway around the world—just to look at this abandoned property with three structures on it. I was intrigued by this rickety house tucked away in the jungle, which happened to be where I had a dream and prayed on the shore of Lake Izabal years prior.

We loaded up into an old van, and after a long journey, we pulled into the village of Ensenada. I said to Otilio, our driver, "Pull over. I want to pray." This was slightly irritating to my husband because it was a very long drive. At the moment, we were stuffed into the van like canned sardines with no cool breeze of an air conditioner. Myself, Jeff, Bert, Ted, and Luis had beads of sweat dripping down like crazy because it must have been one hundred degrees out, but it was dry heat and not raining! We prayed and asked God for a sign, a story.

We continued on to the village and stopped at a chain-link gate. Laundry was hanging from tree to tree and draped all over the fencing, making the yard look like a Chinese laundromat. The mud was ankle deep for us humans, but there were chickens, turkeys, and pigs running all about in my beautiful dream for this property. I had a sobering moment. I looked at the main house—the best one of the three structures standing on the property—and it was totally falling apart. I felt exasperated. However, my friends were walking around with a good attitude. I walked over toward the water where there was an abandoned boat turned upside down under a broken tiki house. It had no roof over a totally cracked concrete floor. I quietly lay down, agonizing on the old boat, and closed my eyes, thinking of the scripture that reads, "Do not exasperate your children" (Colossians 3:21).

But God, I am exasperated! As a dark cloud came over me, I was thinking, *What have I done? I have dragged my friends halfway around the world. I am so, so sorry God. What was I thinking?*

My good Guatemalan buddy Luis, who never fails, came up to me and told me a story. At that moment, he sounded like a pesky fly that I just wanted to swat. I really wanted him to go away and leave me alone. Finally, I heard him as I came out of the depths of despair, feeling one thousand feet deep in the ocean. I looked at him, and I listened to him as he was telling me that a baby girl was born and had been abandoned on the property. He shoved this newborn baby right in my face. My eyeballs must have bulged out of my head.

He said, "Gail, look!"

I was in such a daze. God, in this moment, confirmed every doubt I had just entertained as a lie. This truly was the right property. The baby was abandoned right there by a young woman from Livingston. She just came to the village one day, gave birth, and then left the baby in the arms of the woman taking care of the property. The baby was being cared for by the caretaker, who always wanted a daughter; they would continue to live on the property for the next year. This turned out to have a happy ending. The baby was named Melanie. Eventually she moved with her new family into the village. They live in a nice house where she is dearly loved and cherished.

Life is a series of events, some logical, but others make no sense at all. I realized then that we needed to buy this property because we found the right place, God's choosing. When you're doing God's business, you have to have faith—sometimes more faith than you actually have. It's just like money. In the world, you always need more money. Everything comes with a cost. God's kingdom is built by faith. We are continually challenged to increase our faith. Faith without works is dead (James 2:17) because faith is seen in action.

God loves faith, and God is faithful. The Bible says that the faith of a mustard seed will move mountains and move trees (Mathew 17:20; Luke 17:6). I have heard preachers say, "Count the cost." So now I needed to negotiate with the owner and do some math. I was learning about God's school of accounting.

Peace exuded from this particular property to a high degree. When we walked through the gate, the presence of the Holy Spirit was perceptible. Seriously, we did our homework and looked at many properties, comparing many prices. Everything kept sending us back to this property. It wasn't the cheapest, and it wasn't the easiest; but it was the best for the children, and God's children deserve the best. He gives back what the devil steals, and much has been stolen from these children.

The negotiation went on for months. I had a number in my mind and a Father in heaven. Luis arranged for me to meet with the owner, a kind gentleman from Guatemala City. We met at the restaurant located at the entrance of Agua Caliente. Agua Caliente is a beautiful, cascading, hot waterfall tucked away in the jungle near the town of El Estor. We sat at a long table because I happened to have a mission team with me. I was way outside of my comfort zone. Honestly, I felt like I was bluffing my way through a poker game. I had never negotiated on a piece of property before especially in a language that I don't speak and without the needed funding already in place. However, I knew that if I kept looking at what I didn't have, I'd never do anything.

My Father in heaven owns all the cattle on every hill (Psalm 50:10). He promises to provide for all our needs. On that day, I kept hearing many dump trucks go by. I never heard so many trucks drive by in my life. God spoke through those trucks, and it made me laugh. I kept seeing money going to the bank for this children's home of which I had been dreaming. It's his plan and his house. I want you to know that God is continuously building the house. I am not able, but with God, all things are possible. This house is built on faith and the power of the Holy Spirit. It is a testimony to the truth written in his Word.

Just as with the disciples, you know you're the right person for the job when you know you're the least likely person the world would choose. God has a plan and a purpose for your life to prosper you in his kingdom (Jeremiah 29:11). Somehow our lives blend with the Spirit so that the world we live in becomes a fused reality. Our bodies live in a physical dimension while the spirit is intangible with our hands, but it is just as real and solid when built on the rock of Jesus Christ.

Eventually, the owner and I came into a price agreement. We proceeded to close on the property—that process took an entire year. Little did I foresee the mounds of paperwork ahead of me. Navigating Guatemalan bureaucracy requires a lot of waiting, so if you want to learn patience, come here, but I will tell you it can be painful.

In January 2015, after a few years of fundraising and wiring a ton of money into a Guatemalan bank account, I stepped into the office of my lawyer, whom I had just met. Faith, trust, and Luis were by my side. I thought to myself, *If this doesn't go right, I'm never going to be able to go back home.* There I was with three Guatemalan men in some law office somewhere in Puerto Barrios, a rough and dangerous town. I had no clue what they were saying or what I was signing. I had faith and prayed for mercy. I could only hope Luis was translating well and that I was understanding this contract because I had never bought property in Guatemala before. I was also grateful to have Bert on the phone who was bilingual to aid me in the transaction as well. There is a first for everything.

Remember what I said about patience? I did not know all the mountains of paperwork which had awaited me. It also took a year to legalize Blue Water Surrender as an International Ministry in Guatemala. I was faced with standing in front of my supporters in faith, continuously asking for money to bring a vision into reality, which became a huge challenge to my heart. Year after year, they too had faith as they waited with me, praying and continuing to give with finances and words of encouragement. I guess they were learning patience too.

My faith has been increased by observing and experiencing how God opens doors, step by step, one obstacle at a time. Gaining our legal status gave us the right to apply for a license to have a registered children's home in Guatemala. To carry out this vision has had many complications. I have thought to myself, *Maybe I might want to go back to my simple life of windsurfing in the Florida Keys.* My faith—without research—has gotten me into this adventure. Although if I had done the research and known what it entailed, I probably would not have even tried.

You have heard the saying, "Be careful what you pray for." I can vouch for the truth of this proverb because the next set of paperwork was the most grueling of my life. We had to apply to the CNA (National Counsel for Adoptions), which is a nonprofit organization in Guatemala that oversees child welfare in Guatemala. They are also under the pressure of the United Nations' regulations. Both entities are intense and detail oriented. I was informed that it has taken other homes five years to complete the process. CNA had a larger stack of uncompleted applications than complete. Regulations in the past were more lenient, so many homes were in operation without too many consequences.

In 2017, during our application process, there was a big fire in the Guatemala City area, a huge tragedy where many children lost their lives at the *Virgen de la Asuncion* home. This was thought to be one of the causes for the United Nations to crack down on Guatemala, changing many regulations and instilling more. This seemed to occur on a daily basis. This heartbreaking event slowed down our application process, but somehow, in a record time of two and a half years, we received our license. Out of all the children's homes in Guatemala, only a small percentage have met the requirements during this time. Blue Water Surrender is the first home to become a legalized facility in the Department of Izabal. When I was researching on the internet about the civil war in Guatemala, I read that Izabal had one of the greatest loss of lives in the massacres during the civil war. Once again, I saw God's hand over the children's home, and my heart was touched deeply by this.

Prior to purchasing the property and renovations, we had a huge gathering at the property with the people of the village including some of the local leaders. I had a dream many months before this event, and I awoke from this dream with a strong impression on my mind. I drew the image in a little book next to my bed. It was puzzling but significant. The image was that of uneven neon green crosses in a sporadic pattern of some type. I didn't understand this dream and soon put it out of my thoughts. I had too much to do for me to ponder an incomprehensible image just then.

I was clueless about planning and hosting this whole event. I am grateful to have had Christi, Rachael, Sina, Tracey, and the rest of the mission team by my side. Pastor Antonio's church from town came with a band and more than a hundred people from the village arrived and we began singing songs of praise to God. As the event progressed, the event became overwhelming in a positive way. Have you ever been at a loss for words? Thank God for His Holy Spirit through whom God revealed his heart in a very prophetic way.

I had previously made a storytelling poster to share at a children's church event. It had stars and clouds depicting heaven in the background; it had a very ethereal, dreamy feel. Mission plans change often, and the poster was just waiting to be used. So at the gathering on the property, I decided to post it on the shed door of the very broken-down-but-loved house we wanted to buy. At some point during the service, I asked Pastor Antonio to sign the poster as an agreement to be our spiritual covering here in Guatemala. Then I asked Luis to sign as father to the children, and then I signed. This sounds strange, and to tell you the truth, it is, but my heart was moved to do this. Small actions have the ability to bring great meaning. In that moment, I felt as if I just signed a legal contract in heaven to oversee this house for the children with God as my witness.

Meanwhile, the music continued to play. People were dancing, and this one lady kept pushing her young daughter at me. I didn't know what she wanted; I was confused by her action, and it became somewhat aggravating. I was wondering, *What does she want?* A thought came to my mind. It was the story of the ten young virgins with their oil lamps. With this in my mind, I was thinking of the purity which would be in her prayers, and I placed the young girl's hands, along with two other young girls' that were standing next to her, on the door which now had the poster on it. The door was nailed shut, but suddenly it opened. The people were astonished and made a loud roar! It appeared to be some sort of a sign to them in the spirit. They wanted me to speak.

A crowd gathered in close, and I was being encircled. The reason I was there and had called this very meeting was to ask them permission to come into their village. If they didn't want me here, I wouldn't come. I shared with them that this was not going to be built by money but by faith; if they wanted a move of God, then we would come.

As the meeting came to a close, the people all lined up in a very long line. I felt like I was at a wedding and I was the bride. Everybody hugged me down to the very last one, giving congratulations with exhilarated joy. The next day, my neck hurt so badly from the many hugs. I looked out after all the people had left, and there across the yard were these sporadic neon green crosses glowing in the dark. I was seeing my dream! I was truly amazed to see this scene. Prior to the event, while we were tying glow sticks together with string to make crosses and hanging them on the fence and in the trees, I didn't recall my past dream. What I was seeing at that moment brought it all back, and I was astonished by the prophetic force of it.

Then while we were winding down from the event, I saw an elderly man remaining, sitting in a chair. My jaw dropped—he looked just like my grandfather! I felt like God had sent my grandfather to me. I realized he was the elder of the village, so I stood in front of him, telling him that I wasn't going to come to this village unless he gave me his blessing. I wasn't taking no for an answer. I thought of Isaac and Jacob, and I wanted a father's blessing, which I did receive. Back at the hotel, with a successful gathering and several prophetic occurrences behind me, I was astonished by the people who showed me such great love. I felt welcomed by a multitude!

Moving forward, there was much to rejoice about. Permission had been granted! Papers were signed! Property has been purchased! No debt or mortgage was on the property—it was 100 percent paid! Now it was time for renovations. I thought I had a headache before, but I soon realized we were only now just getting started. There I was—an American woman, head of construction, directing macho men. Double the trouble! It was hard, but I really loved working with the people. I learned so much, and there is so much more to learn.

Annie and Eric, sailors whom I met in the Bahamas, had the pleasure of the first renovation project. First, we cleaned up the house, removing debris because it had been abandoned for years. On the third floor, the deck was in need of rebuilding and looked like a good place to start. I gave Luis the lumber order, and he went off to town to retrieve the necessary construction materials. If I needed something, Luis wouldn't rest until he found it. I must have worn him out many times. He called me from town and explained they didn't have the wood I was looking for. I asked him then to just bring the same type of wood in whatever was available. He returned with four different types of wood with a variety of lengths and thicknesses. Eric had his work cut out for him, but he was determined to have a positive outlook with such a large challenge. The only tools he had were a circular saw and a hammer.

Construction is new for me to start with, never mind learning about Guatemalan jungle construction. For some reason, my head frequently hurt.

A friend on a mission team one time said to me, "Gail, I've had some experience at the lumber yard. Maybe I can help you."

I replied, "Mary Alice, I don't think you understand."

Eventually, she did comprehend when the lumber came to us on the back of an old truck and in place of a tape measure, we used a string to measure circumference. That was a technique I had never seen before, and it startled me; I wondered what I was getting into. I didn't know much about lumber myself, so I was grateful for my friend's help. The lumber at that time was rough cut with a chainsaw, still green from the jungle. I did know you need to build with dry lumber, and your boards should be the same thickness, but it wasn't working that way. Again, I heard Jimmy in my mind, saying, *Don't fight the river.* Fighting the river here only gets you more frustrated. Creative thinking is a must; add in patience to listen to very long explanations, so be certain you have plenty of time. This will help you persevere in the process.

A TRAIL OF THE HOLY SPIRIT

One of my favorite days during this construction season was with Jerry. There was an old outhouse close to the waterfront, and I really wanted something prettier to look at. Jerry dumped some gasoline down in the hole and lit a match, and the whole thing crumbled. Then all I had to do was to get our neighbor, Gerson, to shovel up the debris and wheel it away. What a joyful day! I was so happy to look out and see just the lake.

The day I was really looking forward to turned into the day I cried in confused disbelief. We had purchased the property and were in the process of renovations. With our location on the shores of lake Izabal, one of the largest lakes in Guatemala, you would not think it would be so hard to get water. When it rains here, it really *rains*. You know the saying "It's raining cats and dogs," but here it's elephants—sometimes for days on end. With a lake and so much rain, piping running water to a house still was not a simple task. The village that loves us so much—after much debating and a few dollars—decided they would hook us up to the village water system.

To this day, I don't know why they had been refusing us access to their water. In Guatemala, you need to store your water someplace safe, which was also a new concept in my mind. At home, I just turned on the faucet, and it worked—hot and cold. A cistern was needed. You can have a plastic one or build a cement one; this is the first decision you will need to make before you decide where you will put the monstrous thing. We had discussed the best place for a cistern literally for months. The cistern was finally dug after a generous heart funded the project. The only problem was that they put it in the wrong place—smack dab in the middle of the garden—and cut down my favorite tree at the same time. I made some people nervous that day because they have never seen me lose it. The garden was very important to me. I had been planting flowers for a good reason. I had read *The Hiding Place*, Corrie ten Boom's autobiography. She shared how the garden brought healing to the German soldiers, and I wanted this for our children. The garden was just starting to take off, with beautiful flowers blooming. Yes, I did eventually apologize, but it took some time. Believe it or not, after that heartache, I was so looking forward to flushing the toilet. We had been carrying buckets from the lake to the second floor for way too long, so when I went to flush the toilet and it didn't work, I was disappointed and perplexed. I was told there was no water in the village. Infuriated, I asked Luis and the contractor, "Why then did we build the cistern and pay the village to hook up the water pipe!" Maybe keeping that outhouse would have been a good idea. The issues never ceased to boggle my mind. The only logical thing to do at that time was to cry. With only two inches of water in the cistern, it took weeks before the water rose to an acceptable level to properly run the pump. It took me a while to forgive and move on.

The list goes on and on. I learned a valuable lesson from Marcos, a talented local carpenter whom I love dearly. He was building bunk beds for us, and I was quoted a certain price, remembering to count the cost and be wise. The beds turned out beautifully, but when I went to pay the bill, there were all these other things added on. Needless to say, I was confused. I didn't know it was standard procedure to be charged for the nails that held the beds together plus other miscellaneous items which were needed. That really threw me for a loop. I still don't understand the Guatemalan system. I continue to try to think of everything that would be needed to build something to get one complete price. I have not been able to accomplish this yet, but it has become a goal to attain. I keep attempting, and one day, I will have the victory. If you would like to try, good luck. I am just giving you a heads-up.

Building in the jungle forced me to face many fears. When I moved to the Florida Keys many moons ago, I was introduced to scorpions. Eventually, I became accustomed to them. As time went on, my fear began to waver and, eventually, dissipated. Then sharks raised my heartbeat, but after a couple of encounters, I learned to relax; it is very rare to die from a shark attack. In Guatemala, spiders and snakes are abundant, and many of the snakes are deadly. When I was young, spiders sent me into hysterics, but Guatemalan children played toss with a tarantula and swim with the alligator on our shore. Luis saw a poisonous snake slither up the railing one night—his machete took care of that! We have had snakes sneak in under the door and wiggle across the floor. A snake was even found resting in the kitchen cupboard among our supplies. I finally learned, as I looked around, that typical jungle construction leaves room for ventilation, and ventilation leaves room for critters to enter.

After the house restoration was complete, jungle style, we found a few glitches. A heavy rain poured down from the heavens, causing two inches of water on the floor of the house. The ground is mainly clay and the absorption is slow and when wet, we were ankle deep in muck, and then when the clay dries, it's hard as concrete. A soil percolation test would have given us a heads-up to this challenge.

With the house already existing on the land, one would assume it was in a good place. My brother, who transports horses for a living, once told me, "In this business, assume nothing." I will say the same thing for Guatemala—assume nothing, expect the unexpected, and pray about everything.

In addition to the snakes and spiders, bats have also found a home with us and live in our roof. I have evicted them many times, but they just will not listen. Our many attempts to seal up the gaps have failed. People remind me bats are good because they eat mosquitoes. We have plenty of mosquitoes along with fire ants, beetles, and a variety of creepy-crawling insects I have never seen before. Our friend Bruce says, "Coexist!" I agree to a certain point—I love nature, but prefer it to be outside. The house spoke to us in the beginning and has such spirit and history, but in hindsight, it would have been easier to tear the house down and start from scratch.

Despite everything that has transpired through the struggles and the blessings, I believe we are standing on a firm foundation from our village relationships to our construction projects, even out to the garden. I look at the birth of Casa Agua Azul as a painting. When something goes far different than imagined, it is an opportunity to be more creative and visualize what the next stroke of the brush will be. The Japanese art of *Kintsukuroi* repairs pottery with silver or gold lacquer according to the philosophy that the object is more beautiful for having been broken, so it is in God's world. When something disturbs you, your heart shows what resides within. God is looking to deposit gold in our hearts, but oftentimes, we have to be "Gracefully Broken," as the song by Tasha Cobbs Leonard says.

Trials and tribulation are the process used to bring forth the gold. The creation of Casa Agua Azul required the blending of three very different cultures: American, Indigenous, and Spanish Guatemalan. We all have something to offer each other in our ways of faith, living, and thinking, yet working together can be challenging. Thus, forgiveness is essential to move forward, yielding beautiful fruit, which will remain throughout generations. What is passed on with my hands is nothing of value if my heart has not passed on love to my brothers and sisters. My heart has grown, and I have been blessed to work alongside so many wonderful people. I am filled with awe of them for many reasons especially when I see what is handcrafted from the nature that surrounds us; each piece reflects the heart and soul of the craftsman which will never compare to the work of a machine.

The many modern conveniences we take for granted in the USA are not always present here. In a world crisis, I believe Guatemala will have an advantage over America because the people can live off their land. We as a culture, with all our modern technologies, have moved away from the land as far as tilling the soil goes. In the Florida Keys, in particular, it would be difficult to live off the land—there are only so many coconuts and fish. To live well in the jungle, you're going to need a machete and learn a totally new lifestyle. I love and admire the people in this land for their ingenuity and their connection to the earth. It is a blessing to witness their joy, their value for family and friends, and most of all, their love for God. There is much gold in their hearts, which is a treasure.

Early Construction

5

The Mission

Gaby and I were sitting in the office at Casa Agua Azul on March 19, 2020. Baby Gail was strongly smiling that day despite what was happening in the world. We just received the report of the first case of Corona in the Rio Dulce, which is near the house. We figured it was probably not a good idea, as an American, to go outside of the gates of the property. I felt like a pedigreed poodle that's trespassing while the dog catcher was looking to capture me and place me into quarantine. Next, I received a text notifying me of an update from the State Department recommending Americans "in countries where commercial departure options remain available" to "arrange for immediate return to the United States unless they are prepared to remain abroad for an indefinite period." The airport had been closed for days in Guatemala.

"I guess that's not an option for me," I muttered.

I was wondering if my friends back home were *really* my friends because they kept saying that I'm right where I am supposed to be. Easy to say when you are home with your family and loved ones while the world is going berserk. Seriously, I am grateful for their faith and their support. I love my friends; I prefer not to leave home without them. Regardless, God is good and is guiding us all in our journey of life.

That day, I did not go into the village, but I was able to take the children out for a boat ride on the lake. Feeling the wind and just being surrounded by the water made me feel like I was at home. Being cooped up in the house was not helping my mental state. I never in my life wanted to be separated from my husband and family in a crisis, but there I was, in a world crisis, facing one of my greatest fears. It was a hallelujah moment, for I was just fine. I was grateful to have a supportive husband sending me beautiful texts and to be able to communicate because surprisingly, the Internet connection had been working! It's so surreal.

This alien virus was spreading over the world, killing many people. Every day the reports were coming in. When I heard El Salvador was infected with their first case, it just messed with my mind. I was not able to comprehend what was happening. I felt like I was in a scientific, futuristic movie just as Gaby was feeling like she was in a kids' story book. I hoped this story would have a good ending. The start was great, but the chapter we were in was getting eerie. Yet as I looked around, all was well.

Thinking back to when I was a child, I remember my mom would pray, "God bless all the children in the world." This simple, pure prayer planted a seed and was revealed in what I will call a prophetic dream. In the dream, years ago, when I had started going to Guatemala, I was sitting in a car with my mom at a waterfall; it appeared as if the waterfalls were just up the street from here. I knew in my heart that God was answering her prayer. Along with my mom and through my friends, the nine women in the jungle, I see the great strength God has placed in women. A mother's heart will not be defeated, for love holds strong. The strength of love is a powerful weapon, a driving force.

Our mission is to love. Love comes from one place—love comes from God and belongs to God. A heart beats, and as it beats to love, there is nothing greater. I can feel this in my chest, and it is not of my own, yet it is bursting forth as an unseen, determined force which will never give up.

Over the years, many people have stepped forward to help our mission, compelled by love. Love is contagious and attracts more of the same. People from all walks of life and from all over the world have been finding their way to Casa Agua Azul. Each is an integral part of a beautiful story being written to advance the mission of love.

Our unwavering desire is to create a safe place for the abandoned and abused children who will be entrusted to us through the court system of Guatemala in the loving hands of our caregivers, visitors, and workers. To achieve this goal, we will need to start with love and continue in the flow of love because we care for and respect all as God's unique creation. Our desire is to always remember grace. We are here to build up and not tear down. It is important to be patient, positive, and encouraging. Forgiveness is crucial for all relationships alongside constructive criticism, when necessary, and the avoidance of any shaming, blaming, or unnecessary pain. Another aspect of love is the responsibility to use the funds entrusted to our organization with integrity in keeping with the intention of the donation. We are to act as God has gifted each one of us, maintaining harmony by respecting healthy boundaries. In life, there are so many gray areas, but we would rather serve in full color and transparency.

God is on a mission of love. Our hearts are constantly being tested as the fire purifies, looking for the gold. This is not the same gold that Judas was looking for. He reached for the gold of the earth, betraying Jesus for it, so he never received the true gold of God. God's gold is what is eternal and what will remain. God's gold comes from a deep place—just as gold is mined deep from the earth. A miner digs deep for days on end before he will strike that rich vein. So it is with God. This process can be painful. The end product, as in *Kintsukuroi*, becomes more beautiful.

Pain comes in the most vulnerable moment, often so close to the finish line. Victory is near, but your sweat, your prayers, your life, and your heart are screaming, and then part of you begins to die. Shock and disbelief come. You have a choice—are you going to stand? What is your core? What do you value? Will you stand for your faith? The refining fire is ablaze. Have you faced this fire and found yourself in the dark night of the soul? When all is black, when all is silent and your last fiber of faith is about to be cut, where do you go? This is when you see the one who is your God. Who have you made the God of your life? The call is to surrender—surrender even more to the deep as it is calling. Without the Lord, I have found I am absolutely nothing; but with the Lord, I am everything.

The deep blue of the ocean is significant to us because we are avid sailors. Our organization is named Blue Water Surrender for this very reason. What has captured our hearts is Psalm 82:23:

> Defend the cause of the weak and fatherless;
> uphold the cause of the poor and the oppressed.

Our goal is to provide a stable long-term home where abandoned and abused children will be loved, cared for, educated, and have the opportunity to become well-adjusted productive members of society. Our ministry is Christ-centered for the purpose of rescuing these precious children with the love of God. As I strive toward this goal, I have had to surrender as if I were diving into the depths of the deep blue sea beyond where light penetrates. The depth of the ocean is beyond what I can see; I need to continue to trust and walk by faith.

In Guatemala we receive many strict governmental regulations but no governmental financial support. We are here because of generous hearts who have supported this vision and mission. The impact on the lives of the children has been tremendously positive. We are so grateful, and we cherish in our hearts those who stand with us to fight hunger, pain, and suffering, replacing it with joy, love, and hope.

While my daily attention is primarily focused on Casa Agua Azul, my heart, in writing this book, is to encourage you, as a reader, to step out into greater faith for the kingdom of God. Along with the children in Guatemala, I want you to be part of my story in heaven. This is why I share things close to my heart that God has planted and watered.

A mission is an important assignment to be carried out, and we all have a mission. Our lives prepare us for what is to come. Be anxious for nothing—Moses was forty years old when his life opened up. God has the perfect time prepared in advance. Your life's purpose may still lie hidden within your heart, but in the proper time, it will come forth. We are called to patient endurance throughout our lives, often to wait and to wait even longer; but while we wait, we cultivate expectancy within. Just think of Sarah and Abraham waiting for decades until having a baby was seemingly impossible—but nothing is impossible with God.

In the waiting, keep the fire burning. If you see a bucket of cold water coming your way, duck from the naysayer. Surround yourself with those who will increase your faith. Your thoughts and feelings are important. The hard work is to align your thoughts, feelings, and heart with the truth. Truth comes from the heart of God, written in the word of God. His Word is a lamp to our feet and life to our bones. Remember that what you do is important and what you do not do is also important.

Keep in the forefront of your mind:

> Love is patient, love is kind. It does not envy, it does not boast, it is not proud. It does not dishonor others, it is not self-seeking, it is not easily angered, it keeps no record of wrongs. Love does not delight in evil but rejoices with the truth. It always protects, always trusts, always hopes, always perseveres. Love never fails. But where there are prophecies, they will cease; where there are tongues, they will be stilled; where there is knowledge, it will pass away. (1 Corinthians 13:4–8 NIV)

The heart is what matters, but we have many choices about where we place our hearts. It is what comes out of it that makes or breaks us. Choice is our friend when we choose well, but at the same time, it can quickly become our enemy.

Often we may be living on autopilot with absolutely no awareness of our very own hearts. So many people are disconnected. We live in a fallen world where bad things happen to good people, so we need to live life on life's terms, which means you may have to accept the things you cannot change. As time passes, if we have not accepted this reality, the disappointment and hurt can grab hold of you even with the best of intentions. This negative force has an agenda to snatch and capture your passion. It is time to let go of these past hurts. As we begin the process of letting go, we will wake up with fervor, enthusiastic for life and zeal for the things of God. This will allow your heart to live in a new freedom to walk in God's love.

We are here for a purpose! I call to your spirit to come alive—come alive, leap forth and dance to the song of your heart. To all our dormant thinking, I cry, "Wake up!" Endless possibilities are waiting for you to step in faith—one tiny step at a time.

Fear is the enemy of your mission—the what-ifs. Fear is a liar! I love 2 Timothy 2:7 (NKJ):

> For God has not given us a spirit of fear, but
> of power and of love and of a sound mind.

I have had to say this over and over again, and I will continue to speak this truth, for it is my weapon when fear raises its ugly head. Fear is a deer in the headlights, frozen, becoming a perfect target for the hunter. Frozen means without movement; it paralyzes—just what the enemy of our soul desires.

I am certain you have heard "the battle is in your mind." Joyce Meyers is well-known for this phrase as she has written a wonderful book, *The Battlefield of the Mind*. This is true, and we all are in a battle; it is a human condition. The difference between movement and frozenness is in how people fight their battles. Believe it or not, God's Word is the greatest weapon along with praise! I love the song by Michael W. Smith, "Surrounded," in which he sings, "For the spirit of heaviness, put on the garment of praise. This is how we fight our battles." Think about what is written in Ephesians 6:12 (NLT):

> For we are not fighting against flesh-and-blood enemies, but against evil rulers and authorities of the unseen world, against mighty powers in this dark world, and against evil spirits in the heavenly places.

Does this not take a special weapon to fight? I find the answer to be so clear as written in Hebrews 12:4 (ESV):

> For the word of God is living and active, sharper than any two-edged sword, piercing to the division of soul and of spirit, of joints and of marrow, and discerning the thought and intentions of the heart.

So earthly weapons will not win the battle; only spiritual ones will prevail.

I have experienced in my own life the truth of God's Word when I put it into action. It is the opening of your mouth and speaking forth the truth which will move mountains. If this is not an active part of your life, I encourage you to join me and become a mountain mover today!

I did not always believe and have faith. In my twenties, I ran from the things of God into my own demise. My mom, a blessed woman, would send me spiritual writings. I would become angry and throw them in the trash because something within me was repulsed. What was in me was not the Spirit of God, and the truth is it did not even belong to me; but somewhere in my life, I invited it in, whether knowingly or not. We all are vulnerable to falling asleep and waking up in the courtyard of the devil.

Faith and the Word of God were to become my only way out. For this reason, my heart beats so strongly for the things of God because I have a story of crawling out of the pit of darkness, of self-destruction, demolishing all that was to be beautiful and cherished. In great confidence, I say God is very good. His Word is powerful, containing the keys which will unlock the prisoners of Hades. Darkness fell upon me at age twenty-one and remained for many years because of my ignorance—that is my lack of knowledge. Ignorance momentarily may appear as bliss, but in the long run, it is anything but bliss.

Life is a series of events leading us to places unknown. In my late twenties, I got off a bus in Fort Lauderdale just in time to meet an enthusiastic evangelist who shared the Gospel with me to save my life only for me to return to a madman where sin begat sin. My ears heard, but my heart was still adrift. Years later, a dear friend gave me a Bible, and it sat on my shelf, gathering dust. The answers I needed were there, waiting for me, but I didn't let them in. For that to happen, I had to open the book.

For many years, I did not allow myself to hear God calling me. I was standing alone in darkness until one day, in my forties, I called for help because the darkness was consuming me, and I was very afraid. I called on a wise man of God, who opened the Bible and had me read the words of Deuteronomy 18:9–13 out loud for myself. My heart was pierced as the Word shed its light, causing the darkness to have no choice except to leave. It was not without a battle. I needed to repeat the truth over and over again to fill my mind. This was the start of the truth penetrating my heart.

Life is like a painting—it is not all sunny colors. There are many shades of gray which creep into our lives, clouding our judgment, producing darkness. When we allow God to come into our lives, he paints rainbows in a vastness of rich, beautiful color. His brilliance highlights and emphasizes the main object which he is expressing his love for—which is you. That is what I experienced when I finally opened his book.

Simultaneously, a person, who was dying of cancer came into my life. He point-blank asked me what kind of person I was.

My response was "I am a good person."

To my surprise, he said, in a raspy voice due to the cancer in his throat, "I am a sinner," perplexing me to the core.

This wonderful man, Gabe Mahalic, lying on his deathbed, was desperately trying to convey the most important message of life. Days later, he died, and his wife asked me, of all people in the world, to speak at his funeral. I was driving across Alligator Alley with my husband to attend the funeral, and I heard Tony Evans on the radio in his own raspy voice, saying, "I am a sinner saved by grace. Unless you publicly profess the name Lord Jesus as savior, you will not be saved."

My ears were freaking out. The voice on the radio sounded exactly like my friend who had just passed away. I finally heard the message of truth in order to be able to speak the truth. Of all places, I found life and salvation at the funeral of a man who gave his last breath for God.

I came to the understanding and realized we are not fighting other human beings. I believe there are good and evil forces acting on this earth, and the truth will be revealed. Our lives are constantly being bombarded with unseen forces. We each have a body, a mind, and a spirit being affected. We need to say no to the parts of ourselves which desire what is not good. What is not good is not of God. When we participate in what is not good, we eventually will manifest and be characterized by what we have consumed. It is the law of nature which, without Christ, brings death.

But God desires that none would perish. He went to great lengths to provide provision for eternal life. He has great patience and love although we turn our backs on him constantly. Even though we may say no to him, he continues to stand faithfully, saying, "I will never leave you nor forsake you." His love never changes, and his love never fails. His love never gives up on you. To those who say yes, he gives living water which flows from his throne of grace, giving life to the full.

I am thankful he never gave up on me. I had been standing alone in darkness, and out of the darkness came a great light. Jesus set me free. I turned my back to darkness. Flaws and imperfections he does not see. I share with you the truth: Jesus washed me clean. It has nothing to do with race, and it is not about color. It is what resides in my heart, for that is what he sees. Now I live life to its fullest, and my mission is his mission, but there is one who comes to lie, kill, and destroy. We all have a choice about whom our mission, which is our life, will serve.

When we choose well, we have nothing to fear.

> Do you not know? Have you not heard? Have you not understood since the earth was founded? He sits enthroned above the earth... Do you not know? Have you not heard? The Lord is the everlasting God, the creator of the ends of the earth. (Isaiah 40:21–22, 28–29 NIV)

The fact that I want you to glean is that God is real and powerful; even though you may not see him with your earthly eyes, he is here.

I love these following words. They are filled with power. In his love, God is still just, and he comes against the darkness of evil.

> Please listen, I saw heaven standing open and there before me was a white horse, whose rider is called Faithful and True. With justice he judges and makes war. His eyes are like blazing fire and on his head are many crowns. He has a name written on him that no one knows but himself. He is dressed in a robe dipped in blood and his name is the Word of God. The armies of heaven are following him, riding on white horses in fine linen, white and clean. Out of his mouth will come a sharp sword with which to strike down the nations. He will rule them with an iron scepter. On His robe and on His thigh he has this name written, "KING OF KINGS AND LORD OF LORDS" (Revelation 19:11–16 NIV)

There is victory in Jesus for those who believe; it is a choice. With Jesus, you surrender to win, for he is love, and in love, justice will be found as his mercy and grace prevail.

> For he disarmed the powers and authorities,
> He made a public spectacle of them, triumphing over them by the cross. (Colossians 2:15 NIV)

Have you made your final choice? I have, and I never want to go back or change my mind, for life in Christ is truly life everlasting.

A dream realized

6

The Children

In the village of Ensenada, the Corona story continues as four foreigners, thought to be either Russians or Americans, were taken from El Estor into quarantine. The more remote an area is, the more suspicious people are of outsiders. We've experienced similar troubles many times through the years. Jerry and Griselda are reluctant to let me, Mama Gail, outside the compound; they are concerned someone will take me away. Some days I need a quick walk down to the shoreline, and on those days, Jerry assigns Marlon to be my bodyguard. If the officials were to come and take me away, he could run back with a message. Today we have a greater health concern with Baby Gail. Her condition has gotten worse. She is just screaming in tears of pain. Since she is under the jurisdiction of the government, it is mandatory for her to go to the hospital in Puerto Barrios. Jerry thought it was best for Blanca to accompany him especially if Baby Gail had to remain in the hospital, which is a fearful thought. Eight hours later, they returned with Baby Gail, praising God for his goodness. A visit to the hospital scares me. I hear that song "Hotel California" again—you can check in, but you wonder if you will ever leave.

The virus is causing many missionaries serving in Guatemala to be stranded, just as I was; but in some cases, it was working out to our advantage. Jay, a missionary from "Water Mission," had read our Facebook post asking for help with our water system and pump. Our answer to prayer that stressful morning traveled two and a half hours from Poptun, passing through roadblocks to come and help us out. This was a very risky move as we were all unsure he could even return to his mission base as roads were shutting down all over the interior. I was so grateful to be able to soap up our hands and have running water to rinse with especially with it being a suggested precautionary measure for good health against the Coronavirus.

Since I left Florida, I was believing God was going to do something great on this trip, and he had! The Spirit seemed to keep pushing me to be here. I pressed on in faith, never expecting a pandemic to fall upon the earth while I was here. I love the faithfulness of God; he sent Jay to stay for a while and become part of our Casa Agua Azul family. God always sends help. The question is not *Why am I here?* The fact is I am here, and I have a purpose!

Many decisions needed to be made at the house. It was good I was there to be of help. God had also sent Gaby to be with us at this time. After working very hard one day, we needed to collapse somewhere quiet. Gaby and I decided to walk down the beach with our assigned bodyguard to go for a swim. The day before, we had taken the kids out on the boat, and we saw a giant alligator in the water. My eyeballs just bulged out of my head; the gator was seriously mammoth, not a cute little one. So now before we were to get in the water, we took a very good look around. It took me a while to get comfortable with sharks back in the Florida Keys, but now the challenge of alligators was in my face. They don't seem to bother the local villagers, but I am still not comfortable. Jumping in, our toes hit the hidden seaweed—a little scratchy but oh so refreshing the beautiful mountains in our view.

Reflecting on what was happening in the world, I shared my heart with Gaby. This was a moment in time when anxiety was floating in the air looking for a place to root. I had been traveling back and forth to Guatemala for many years—often alone, separated from my husband, feeling a bit nervous at times when there is talk of a civil war, roadblocks, political unrest, mudslides, and closed borders. When you think about the end times, it's easy to see the birth pains and hear the footsteps of Jesus. The funny thing is I feel so much peace and joy. I feel the hand of God touching with a blessing.

Even though I am apart from my husband, I feel so much closer to him from our rich conversations, and I'm grateful when the Internet works to receive more of his beautiful supportive texts. My heart is lifted when a friend takes the time to encourage me by email or to send out a loving text and the occasional phone call. Love strengthens us for any journey that is ahead.

Finishing our swim, Gaby and I noticed the contractor working on the little house near the lakefront. We walked over to meet him and have a conversation. Gaby is a wonderful translator, and without her, many of our accomplishments would never have come into being. It's the first house I've seen in this area that is sealed off to bugs and varmints. Here is a quality contractor in our area that we so desperately need. I considered this a miraculous moment! God is here.

As we continued home, we stopped on the side of the soccer field where earlier a giant tree had crashed down; we wanted to take a look to see what happened. The tree was monstrous, and for some reason, it just tipped over. Thank God no children were playing on the field at that time. Gabriella, a young friend of ours who is eleven years old, came out to greet us. It had been a while since we had seen each other, so we spent some time chitchatting while we looked at the tree. Gabriela said she was fasting.

I asked her, "What kind of fast?"

She said, "Nothing."

I did not understand at first. She explained that she and her family, along with the entire church, were fasting for six days, consuming nothing, not even water. I was astonished by their hearts sold out to God, practicing what they believe, which is the power of prayer and fasting. I admire how the people of the village rely on God and find peace in him despite the unknown in the world.

Throughout this time in Guatemala, I have been pondering this strangeness I kept sensing in the atmosphere. As much as I felt exceptional peace, it also felt as though little creatures were just waiting for an opportunity to pounce on me through my thought life. It would increase when I would go onto Facebook and read what others were posting and look at what was going on around the world.

What I would read intensified the negative. We as people appear to gravitate downward, speculating as if the bad news was sweet as honey. In contrast, with the naked eye and the ear void of the news, I could see so much of God's love surfacing. People lined up for action; for once, mankind appeared as if he was unified and ready for war—not among each other but for the preservation of the human race. Governments were closing borders rapidly. They were patrolling and protecting their borders as the effects of the virus were all unknown at this time, and many lives were being lost around the world. Businesses were shut down for public safety. What we knew as ordinary life was drastically changing, with multitudes of restrictions being instated. Nevertheless, I am able to see love being revealed, but mankind does not like feeling controlled, and freedom was being taken away. Watching the governments around the world react, I was overwhelmed by God's love, moving me to tears. Each country was coming for its own people to bring them home; I envisioned this action as a good father who protects and sacrifices for his family just as it is with our God.

Another good father is our director of Casa Agua Azul, Jerry Makepeace, and his lovely wife, Griselda. They were handpicked by God because they are the most loving parents with the ability to bring restoration into the hearts of the children. Working alongside them, we have a full staff which consists of a doctor, psychologist, social worker, teacher, nannies, our superstar Mama Blanca, along with a groundskeeper. All of these workers are required by law to keep a healthy, safe environment for the children. Our staff is numerous to meet the many extra needs which come with caring for vulnerable children.

You never know what's going to happen when you're running a children's home in Guatemala. We have precious moments, funny moments, hair-raising moments, and some really crazy times. A three-ring circus is tame compared to some days at the house. When we received our first children, I was surprised any of us survived. There was crying, screaming, little ones going out in the yard at two o'clock in the morning to eat mangoes, and children bouncing off the walls in chaos. Given the circumstances, this is normal. The children have not had the experience of much or any discipline in their lives. Many of them have been beaten or left to roam the streets. They have had to hide, take care of themselves, and depend only on themselves to survive. They are taken away from their parents during a crisis, processed by the law, then brought to us in a police car. We are strangers to them, far away from their home. They usually arrive in the middle of the night, which makes matters worse. Many tears accompany the fear in their eyes when they arrive. It is extremely intense.

I remember back to March 2019, our first children arrived after years of building and waiting. In my heart, I heard the words of 1 Peter 1:7 (NIV):

> These have come so the proven genuineness of your faith, of greater worth than gold, which perishes even though refined by fire, may result in praise, glory and honor when Jesus Christ is revealed.

I really felt the refining fire when we received our first children as I was here at Casa Agua Azul with Jerry and Griselda. It was insane. I had raised one son. He was very gentle and compliant in nature. To spend twenty-four-seven at the home and really experience what's going on is an eye-opener. We get up early, and we go to bed late. It can be nonstop all day. There is always a building project, something broken, paperwork, responsibilities, groceries, and medical needs for the house mixed in with the emotional needs of the children. I remember one night clearly—Jackie, a missionary from Nicaragua, was at the house, and we all had a very long day. Jerry and I were exhausted but still working in the office. It was close to 10:00 p.m., and my time in Guatemala was rapidly coming to a close. At 5:00 a.m., we would be heading for the airport in Guatemala City, but reconciliation of finances still needed to be completed to ensure proper bookkeeping. Numbers are not my favorite thing to do, but God empowers you in your weakness.

We were exhausted, but then outside of the window came one of our little boys, wailing and wailing, "*Papasito!*" (which is an affectionate way to say "Daddy" in Spanish). Somehow, with a screaming child and the rest of the house still going nuts, we were able to remain calm and do our work with a smile. You learn to give the children what they need when they need it, which is basically at the drop of a hat. In one moment, your mind is deep into important business to sustain the house, but then you may have to deal with a crisis. Better yet is to receive a big incoming bulldozer hug and in the next minute get swarmed by a whole tribe of kids all trying to climb up your legs and arms at the same time. In these moments, God continues to be gracious by giving strength and patience in my weariness and the awareness that each child is a special gift.

The children are wonderful, with tender hearts, but severely wounded. They have all seen things and have experienced heinous acts beyond their years. When a child walks off with the PVC pipe glue while you are in the middle of using it, you better go investigate. To hear a child say, "I wanted to see why my dad would do it" is more than sad as he attempts to repeat the same behavior.

Girls love to dance, and we have some really cute young girls. I pray you have not witnessed a child of six or seven years of age behave like a stripper or young children who are more than curious, hiding in a garden. Children watch and learn. There is so much to be undone, but Jesus is faithful. Jesus has a way of healing; just as he used the good Samaritan, he will use us to bind up the wounded hearts of those exposed to evil. Love never fails.

One of our boys is very concerned about his sister having to possibly go back home. His mom is trying hard to have his sister, who is nine, returned by the judge. He shared how his mom sells her body for money and, prior to being taken away, was teaching his younger sister to pole dance. Unfortunately, months later, the children were returned to their mother. Shortly thereafter, the mother was murdered by a gunshot to the face. This is poverty of spirit and injustice to the children. We do not know much about these children when we receive them. It is through time and conversations, often shared among themselves, when we learn some of their history.

Another one of our boys also shared that his mom sells her body. He had to steal to survive, and his younger brother, at age six, was working in a restaurant so he could eat. Somehow they managed to watch over their youngest brother, who was four. These boys were brutally beaten. One punishment they would receive was to sit in a red ant pile. They have talked about how a cousin was trying to introduce them to manhood in a very ungodly, disturbing way.

These realities do not have to be their future. This is why Casa Agua Azul is here. We are doing everything we can to bring healing to their hearts and tear down the strongholds in their minds from the abuse that they have suffered. We believe in the healing power of an almighty God who is more than able. In Matthew 18:6 (NLT), Jesus said,

> But if you cause one of these little ones who trusts in me to fall into sin, it would be better for you to have a large millstone tied around your neck and be drowned in the depths of the sea.

A heart which is full of compassion must wonder what has led the parent to partake in the demise of their own child. This is unnatural; the innate nature of a mother is to love and nurture her child just as a father protects and provides. It is heartbreaking to see how the natural God-given impulses of a mother or father can become distorted and harmful.

Sergio, one of our children, came down with dengue fever. Dengue is not normally life-threatening, but at certain times in Guatemala, it strikes with greater force than normal. It is carried by mosquitoes, so the rainy season, when water is pooling everywhere, is a dangerous time for the spread of dengue. Also, there are four strains of this infection. Type 2 is the most virulent. In the summer of 2019, type 2 was spreading across Central America including Guatemala. We discovered this after our first family outing for pizza in the Rio Dulce. The kids were eating five to ten pieces of pizza as if they have never been fed before, but Sergio only ate two pieces and was acting nervous. No one could ever have known what was coming next. At the end of the meal, everyone stood up with satisfied grins and laughter, and then Mama Gail had to face one of her greatest fears!

"Oh my goodness, Sergio became very ill to his stomach, similar to when sailing on the high seas!"

It was not good advertising for a pizza place.

We drove back home and discovered that fever had come upon him. He was kept under observation. We had no idea what was really happening to him at this time because children get sick all the time. In the morning, our nanny attempted to prepare him for school, and it was then the red alert appeared. His nose was starting to bleed. I remember my brothers having nose bleeds constantly, so I was not alarmed in this moment; but apparently, it meant something else to Jerry. One of our children was definitely extremely sick. Fingers started moving fast on the telephone screens. God made it possible for our messages to go through as Jerry had left early in the morning and was in sketchy cell range. He received our message and called Doctor G. He then coordinated with the fire departments and the paramedics. It was too far of a distance to waste time. Griselda and Hany put him in the "Bat Mobile," our truck, and hurried him to meet with the paramedics. It was a race for life.

The paramedics wasted no time transferring the child immediately. No questions asked. Along the way, there was a protest and a roadblock where nobody could go through. Thank goodness that Sergio was riding in the ambulance and not in a regular automobile. The ambulance was stopped. People with machetes approached. As the protestors opened all the doors of the ambulance, the paramedics argued on behalf of the child. After a strong hesitation, God's hand moved and made it possible for the ambulance to get through. Sergio arrived at the children's hospital where children were lying on the floor and hospital beds were overtaking the hallways. An outbreak of dengue fever was taking the lives of children, but one bed was still available for Sergio.

Immediately, he was diagnosed with dengue fever. He cried in fear as he saw the girl next to him bleeding to death. The next morning, the cries of another child on his right awoke him only to realize that the child, whose name he had just learned, passed away before his eyes. And then panic invaded. The nanny woke up from sleeping on the floor under Sergio's bed and found Sergio trembling with fear.

A TRAIL OF THE HOLY SPIRIT

Then Jerry came in with no permission whatsoever, went straight to Sergio, patted him on the chest, and said, "Come on! You're my little superman, and the children are asking for you at home."

He stopped trembling, smiled, and started to ask questions about the children at home and Mama Gris. His health was restored! Sergio and his sister stayed with us for six months and then were reunited with their family. Their family has had victory over many challenges, and today they live in a small village near the border of Honduras. As great a miracle as Sergio's healing from dengue was, he has also experienced ongoing joy from forgiving what he felt was unforgivable. His aunt had been cruel and extremely abusive. God's presence in his life is making what looks impossible be possible.

When we receive children in the home, they are court-ordered by the judge to be cared for by us. The mystery of what has happened to them is slowly revealed through things that they say and actions that they take. Looks can be deceptive. We received a twelve-year-old boy once who was a wolf in sheep's clothing. After the fact, we realized the court had pushed this child upon us. He had been going from house to house, leaving a trail of destruction. Your heart can only wonder because your mind cannot conceive of what happened to this child to form him into who he is today. As much as you want to love the unloved, you must protect your other children.

This young man is a sad story. At such a young age, he suffered from psychotic delusions and was sexually abusive to very young children. It was a difficult process to have him removed from the house despite the threat he was to his peers. The authorities were reluctant to aid in any way, so Ted and I housed him temporarily on our boat. We had to guard the door at night so that he would not escape. This child was very smart and slick in language. Finally, for an additional fee, we were able to get a special court date. Standing before the judge, he was court-ordered to a facility which has the infrastructure to contain a child of his nature.

When a child arrives at Casa Agua Azul, it is a delicate situation. For some reason, they usually show up after midnight, escorted by the police. The children are like a stray dog that no one wants—unloved, unwanted, and alone, often suffering from malnutrition, head lice, wounds on their bodies, and crushed spirits. They are scared, not knowing where they are going, as they are placed into the arms of strangers. Prior to arriving, they have usually suffered some final horrific act of violence which brought them here. Rarely do we receive one child at a time; they usually come as a group of siblings huddled together like chicks without a mother hen.

But Casa Agua Azul becomes a haven of safety and rest for each child. A tiny girl, only twenty-nine pounds at the age of two and a half, found hope and healing at the house. She was suffering from malnutrition, could barely hold her head up or sit on a stool at the dinner table. She was extremely despondent, with such sadness on her face. In the beginning, if you looked at her, she would throw herself on the floor and wail; it was absolutely heartbreaking. We do not know what traumas she has suffered, but by continuing to give her love, little by little, she started to communicate.

One day, after receiving flower-patterned sneakers, she walked up to Jerry and said, "*Papasito*, look," and she pointed to the flowers on her dress and how they matched her sneakers. I will never forget the day she first smiled. We were sitting at the table doing selfies and showing them to her. Her little toothless smile broke forth and was worth a million dollars. It was such a victorious moment in time! She also loved the baby chicks. She would carry one around with its belly up like it was her little baby. I believe the nurturing of the baby chick brought much healing to her heart as she held and cared for something smaller than herself. Learning to give and receive love has been healing for her.

All of our children are required to appear at court hearings as the judge decides what is best for the child. After arriving at her court hearing, along with her sister and two brothers, the judicial officials could not believe this was the same child. In such a small period of time, her transformation was like night and day. We were shocked when the judge ordered her and her siblings to be returned to their home. Truth often gets twisted, and lies are told to the judge.

A couple of months later, with the onset of Corona, we received a call from the father asking for help. The law of Guatemala not only places the responsibility to care for the children on us, but it also requires us to counsel the parents while the children are in our care. When a child is returned to his family, we also are mandated to do follow-up visits. Unfortunately, in this case, the children were taken away from the parents again and placed in another home. Our hearts were broken; it was not a surprise but only a matter of time. The writing was on the wall.

Rehabilitation takes time and also willingness. With Corona in full bloom, it would be too risky to the health of the other children to accept them back to Casa Agua Azul. However, our arms were open wide if they would award them to us after the threat of the virus passed. The lesson of letting go is always at work. We do not have a choice but to be obedient to the authorities—in this case the judge. It's not easy once you have a child to care for—in your heart, they become your own, but we have to continually release them. Our job is to be here for them, to love them, to care for them with whatever amount of time is allowed. They are all God's children. We have chosen to believe that the judge and the court system are doing the best that they can with the knowledge that they have. We pray that God will give us all wisdom in the difficult situations that we face. Despite parental abuse, we have noticed that most children love their parents and want to be with them. Our trust must be in the Lord because he loves all the children. It is sin in the world that is hurting these children.

The art of living is making something beautiful out of situations that are unpleasant. Guatemalans are especially great at repurposing things that other people might discard, and so it is with ugly boxes—especially if the ugly boxes are going to be part of your furniture. Life is not about what you do not have in your possession. I say keep life simple—use what you do have. Life becomes an art project to create with what is in your hand.

Often you may have a vision, but God has a better vision. What looked like the ugliest boxes in the world staring us in the face soon turned into an afternoon of love. With a small amount of paint, which was inadequate to cover the old fruit container boxes well, the girls started to paint. We were not able to find our small paint brushes to decorate our ugly half-painted soon-to-be-beautiful clothes containers, but we discovered markers would work just fine. Then eyeing the glue and art sparkles, we had a grand fun-filled finish. Each child was delighted, decorating their own box while listening to music. At the end, Ludwing, who builds many items for us, sprayed a final coat of varnish, and what did we have but the most love-filled, beautiful boxes! Often, our strongest and most essential resources are our relationships. This was our strongest resource in transforming those boxes. We were able to dance and laugh together and make art in the dance of life.

Another dance of life was an encounter with a goat. The story begins with Flori and Hugo, a local couple who live several hours up the lake. They fell in love with the children especially three of the boys who are brothers. Love is needed to load up your horse in your truck and travel a dusty pothole road to spend a day at the Casa, giving all the children pony rides. When Flori and Hugo arrived, Hugo had a baby goat in his arms named Michael, a gift for the house. One of our boys immediately fell in love with it, wrapping his arms around Michael. He was barely able to let this sweet little wide-eyed goat down. Later that night, Jerry checked in on the boys in bed for the night. In the bunk, with his head and hoof on the pillow, was Michael, asleep in the arms of the child. How great is love!

Given the success of animal therapy, we decided to buy more baby chicks for the children. We were starting to notice the healing power the children were receiving from taking the responsibility to care for these tiny fragile creatures. This does not come without complications! The squeals of joy when they saw the little chicks was off the charts. The children love to love. One night, one of our sweet boys put the chicks to bed. Innocently, he grabbed a bucket which was being used to carry concrete at that time; we were building the seawall on the lakefront. Next, he knew the chicks needed water. He put the chicks in the bucket with a small cup of water in the shed for the night. In the morning, Jerry got up to find the chicks encrusted in cement! After washing them, the chicks still didn't look so good. They walked around all day in the sun, still a little crispy. Another bath was needed. We lost a couple of them, but the next day, we had fluffy chicks. You need to always keep your eyes open because children's creativity is unbounded. Accidents are going to happen around children; it is just a matter of how many and how bad.

One time, I was sitting at the table with Jerry and asked how many tortillas a person will typically eat in a day. He answered, "It depends on the culture." We are a multicultural house filled with Latino, Garifuna, and Q'eqchi children. Jerry's opinion is that Q'eqchi eat five to eight, Latinos weigh in at three to four, and at this time, Garifuna was still a mystery. My next question was "How many do our children eat?" Jerry said they provided three tortillas per meal because if they allowed them to eat too many, they could possibly end up suffering. It is wise to raise them up in their culture; otherwise, we will be doing them a disservice. We desire for them to achieve their full potential in life, but if the court decides to return them to the families who have limited resources, including food scarcity, the children will need to be prepared. This is something as an American I would have never thought of.

The same goes for toys and excessive gifts. In some cases, abundance may cause shame. Much of the children's identity comes from their birth family. When we give the children more than what their parents can provide, it has the potential to cause emotional issues. It is important to find a balance. The children have everything they need to be healthy, to be able to learn and to feel loved. Often they are gifted with much from visitors in cakes and fiestas where I can see God giving back what the devil has stolen. For their personal possessions, we monitor the gifts and distribute them in a way to promote positive growth within the child without overindulgence. As much as you want to give everything to these children, in the long run, it would be a disservice.

At the end of the day, like any family, we want to relax and spend some time with each other. One of our favorite things that we love to do is jump in the lake! It is fun to swim around and just be silly, paddle the *cayuco*, which is a handmade wooden canoe, and tell stories and jokes. This is only semirelaxing as with nineteen children or so, your eyes better be open to be a referee, but it is great fun! It is important for the children to experience life beyond basic caregiving. They need to play and relate to one another and learn how to be children—the precious little ones of God the Father. This may be the most important gift we can give them, and it answers my question of "Why am I here?" I see the answer in their faces in so many different ways.

A very loved Goat

7

The Missionaries

God's promise of provision continued during the unknown first weeks of Coronavirus. Rain from heaven fell from the sky, filling the cistern which supplies our director's house. It had been unusually dry a few weeks before. Water is essential for life. I awaken to the sounds of the village music in the distance as it travels across the way the rooster crows. Children are singing hallelujah, making beautiful music to the Lord. Peace is settling over Casa Agua Azul. The dawn of a new day is here.

Jerry had already gone to town to pick up some fresh goat's milk donated to us from Casa Guatemala, another children's home in the area. As I checked my phone, I read the announcement sent out by President Trump for all Americans to return home immediately; otherwise, you must prepare to stay indefinitely. It was a little difficult to immediately follow his instructions. I felt pressured to fill out the form on the US Embassy website with my pertinent information stating I would like to return to the United States.

What appeared to be a simple task became a complicated, frustrating matter due to a weak intermittent Internet signal. Then the phone said, "No service." In my heart, I knew that this would pass, but it was a rather impossible situation. My attitude changed when I looked out the window. The sun was shining through the palm fronds, and it was extremely beautiful. Birds were chirping, and a few raindrops remained. Jerry had returned, and I heard his voice speaking the Word of God to the children while the babies started to cry. Then as he began to pray, they all began to sing. The beauty set before me had brought much peace and perspective.

The children have been learning the power of prayer and decided to fast for the world crisis at hand. At 2:00 p.m., the fast was broken with fresh goat's milk. While sitting at the table, Jerry shared the news report of the day. President Giammattei of Guatemala had said that his face was not pale because he forgot his makeup; it was because he was fasting. They were building hospitals in Guatemala City, Zacapa, Peten, and Xela. He said that he would not be doing his job if he was not protecting his people. At that moment, only seventeen confirmed cases of Corona were in the country who were in need of medical treatment. The reporters asked the president if it was true that he was building mausoleums. He said no. That, by far, that was not true because they were fasting and praying, trusting in a powerful God. It would be in vain that we are not trusting the power of God to answer our prayers; it would be a lie that he is not a strong God.

Dr. G came to check on Baby Gail. He examined her and told us the infection was subsiding. Afterward, he shared with Gaby how we met the first time. He began, "As I was entering through the gate of Casa Agua Azul, I didn't know it was an electric gate." He paused momentarily then continued, "I tried to pull the string that was hanging on the gate doorway, and the gate started moving fast. I didn't know what to do until someone stopped the gate and I was able to get my hand out just before being crushed." He is a great doctor to the children. I was afraid we might have scared him off!

We are not in this world alone. We were designed to live in community. Many will come by your side, and many will also go. To keep our hands and hearts open is to love. Love freely gives unconditionally. If it is anything other, then it is not love. Love is pure, and its only motive is to love. There are many lessons I have learned about love, and many more lie ahead. I am grateful to have companions by my side; this does not always happen. I have traveled countless times alone watching this vision come forth. I much prefer—and love—traveling with friends. Friendships grow through time and through what you experience together. Certain times are just plain great, but other times may be a challenge, which is easier to overcome with a friend by your side. The joy is greater when the victory comes. The unexpected will happen.

The best way to deal with the unexpected is to trust God, pray, and listen to different perspectives as you wait upon the Lord. I have learned there are many ways that good friends help each other to change for the better. I have many cherished memories of the people who have come alongside and served with us. I love to share their stories. Some of my greatest memories have been while traveling with Rachel and Danielle, two friends who have been very active in supporting Casa Agua Azul. Rachel has a background in photography, writing, and social work. She dedicates her summers to assisting our staff and children and leading mission teams. Danielle is a teacher with a dynamic personality. She loves to bring many to the mission field and is always ready for a good adventure! The depth of Rachel's heart and Danielle's vivacity are a winning combination, sure to make you smile.

When we travel to Guatemala from the US, we will usually fly into Guatemala City although San Pedro Sula, Honduras, is also an option. There are times we will travel in from Honduras because it is a shorter route. I like flying into San Pedro Sula for this reason. However, there is a longstanding warning that it is one of the most dangerous cities in the world. I have never felt threatened in this area, but it would not be wise to travel alone or in the dark. Complications arise here due to the border closing at night, making the timing of your flight crucial unless you want to spend the night outdoors. Along the way, you pass by banana plantations and some of the most beautiful wilderness. There are many rivers along this route which, at times, have flooded. When it rains, it really pours. Higher up in the mountains, the rain can cause flash flooding. On many occasions in the past, we have also experienced mudslides, which will shut down the road, causing delay. Often we have been stopped by the police. There are many checkpoints along the way. It is a well-known drug transportation route, so have your passport ready. Central America is always an adventure, but I assure you there are times when everything goes right and you are in a beautiful dream.

I love flying into Guatemala City because we often spend the night at our rooftop camping site, home to Riechelle Rogers, also known as Momma Mish; she is the founder of Faithful Steps Ministry. Riechelle is a medical advocate for the children of Guatemala. She cares for those in San Juan Hospital by improving conditions for patients and parents along with connecting them to medical care, which otherwise would be out of their reach. She is my Mother Teresa of Guatemala City.

Once in Guatemala City, you are only partway to Casa Agua Azul, located in an area called the Rio Dulce. The drive is long as you wind through the coolness of the mountains and travel across farmlands, passing many small villages and towns, eventually entering the hot and humid jungle region. Due to traffic, a six-hour drive may turn into eight hours or more. Traveling the road called the Pan American Highway, or the Trans-Atlantic Road, is one of the most dangerous parts of the trip. The road is two lanes with many trucks traveling between Puerto Barrios and Guatemala City. Despite the close oncoming traffic, impatient drivers will zip in and out, passing slower-moving vehicles. It is quite the experience.

The size of the team we are traveling with will dictate which mode of transportation we use. One economical option is the Litegua Bus Line, a short taxi ride from the airport. For large teams, we hire a private van; and for a small private group, Jerry will pick us up. By the time we reach our destination in the Rio Dulce, it's "good night" to the sun as the night sky takes over with brilliant stars above.

Guatemala is a never-ending wonder from the mountains to the shore. Resting quietly between landforms, Casa Agua Azul is tucked away on the shore of Lake Izabal in the indigenous village of Ensenada. Lake Izabal is the largest freshwater lake in Guatemala and empties into the Caribbean Sea via the grand twenty-two-mile-long river, the Rio Dulce.

To arrive by sea and travel up the river in a boat is the polar opposite of driving in from the city. It is my favorite way to Casa Agua Azul. As you travel up the river, the sound of the jungle becomes a symphony to your ears, with echoes bouncing off vast canyon walls which extend some three hundred feet toward the sky; the walls are filled with lush green vegetation and birds flying overhead. The canyon area is where the movie *New Adventures of Tarzan* was filmed back in 1935. I imagine the filmmakers chose this area for its wild splendor.

The beauty of the Rio Dulce is immeasurable. Along the riverbank is an area where hot springs bubble up, generated from volcanic activity and hillside caves. The river broadens into an area called the Golfete, where the eco-project of Tenamit Maya is located. They offer zip line canopy tours on their resort property. Continuing along the river from high up in the mountains, small tributaries trickle down, pouring forth into the great river where many villages are hidden, and the only access to them is by water.

Life in the jungle never ceases to amaze me. One day while I was relaxing, a chicken was almost flattened by a coconut. I was sitting, looking out at the stillness of the lake, and then *boom!* a coconut fell, and the chicken ran off, squawking. What a strange and noisy death that would be for a chicken! Casa Agua Azul is surrounded by many grand-sized prolific mango trees. When the mangoes start to drop and hit the roof, it sounds like a shotgun going off. Other noises in our jungle neighborhood include the roosters crowing for food and the short squawk of a chicken as it becomes breakfast for the pet alligator next door. Our friend Bruce says we need to coexist with nature. Sometimes I am not sure I agree especially when the ants start crawling on my feet, biting. Our roof is home to bats which refuse to move out, and at night, the ants start marching while the bats start their nightly flights. The mosquitoes think they belong in your bed, disregarding the nets, and they always seem to find your ear. We are praying for a new roof that will not allow bat access.

We like to keep things moving! When a visitor arrives, we like to say, "Let's get rolling!" One can expect the unexpected, and at times, it may feel a bit crazy. Every day becomes a unique adventure. Blue Water Surrender is on mission with the Holy Spirit. You may find our method of mission a bit unorthodox, but as John 3:8 (NIV) says,

> The wind blows wherever it pleases, you hear its sound, but you cannot tell where it comes from or where it is going, so it is with everyone born of the Spirit.

It's just really hard to put God in a box especially in Guatemala. So welcome to the mission field. Let's get rolling!

The many sounds of the mission can be summed up in the phrase "hurry up and wait." This is the most exhausting, hardest part as an American—to *wait*. There is a book titled *Warm Climate, Cold Climate*, which is useful in helping you grasp the things you do not understand while working in a foreign culture. In America we live in an extreme culture, far different from the majority of the world. What is rude or not rude in one culture may not be so in the other and vice versa. The one thing I have noticed is that I like yes or no answers, and that does not work well even in the United States. I am learning to listen, and when you add in a translator to the mix, I am often listening for a long time. I have had to learn patience on top of patience, giving grace to myself and to others.

Some of God's greatest work happens in the waiting. Your heart is being prepared; this is what God is interested in—your heart. It is a great test to see what you are made of. You will learn much about yourself and see who you really are when put under pressure. Are you willing to submit your will to God's will and timing? Will you praise God in the waiting? Oftentimes you will not, and other times you will see how much you have grown. The Israelites complained in the desert, so they waited forty years.

Our attitude is our latitude, and it dictates the future outcome. I firmly believe whatever the circumstances are, good or bad, when we praise God, he will make our path straight, and no weapon formed against us will prosper. Our weapons of warfare are mighty to pull down the defeating strongholds lodged in our minds. Each person must search their own heart and be right with their brother or sister; then you are ready to go out because now you have something to share: the kingdom of God dwelling within.

Pitter-patter! The sound of little feet is the most beautiful sound. I had dreamed of this day for many years. Casa Agua Azul is finally here! There have been many times along this journey that doubt would assault my faith with roadblocks to be bulldozed and mountains to be moved. This moment was long dreamed of by many as the running of many feet raced to the car. Any time you pull into

Casa Agua Azul, the children are jumping with joy, eager to greet you and help carry items into the house.

In the summer of 2019, Jerry picked me and a couple of friends up at the airport and drove us to Casa Agua Azul. On arrival, after being lovingly smothered by many hugs, we unpacked the car, which was filled to the brim. We had supplies from the US, and any empty space available in the car was filled along the way with vegetables. The final squeeze was one last crate of bananas wedged between Daniella and Rachel. It was a long cramped ride from Guatemala City but a joyful one.

We settled in and enjoyed time with the children. The next morning was a time of coffee and planning for the days and weeks to come. It would be a busy summer at Casa Agua Azul with mission teams eager to serve. The sky was clear, and the first thing I noticed was Hany, our social worker, sitting with the children, teaching our youngest ones. What caught my attention, beyond the letters they were learning, was the shapes she was cutting out. The shape of a heart spoke loudly to me and continued appearing through the rest of the day. A heart of love is our main requirement; with this, all else fall into place. Our theme and prophetic word coming forth was the reclaiming of hearts. Suddenly, a loving revelation hit me. As we listen for the Lord, we will hear the heart of God speaking in many forms, giving new ideas and thoughts. That day, as I was listening for direction from the Lord, a thought suddenly came and was snatched out of the air into my mind. It was time for a new project! Our creation today would be a heart-shaped sandbox for the children. If heart restoration is what we're all about, and if you are going to build a sandbox, why would you make it square? Why not make it heart-shaped to reflect the love of God? God is love, and nothing is impossible with God for those who believe. I urge you to listen and hear what God is speaking to you at this very moment.

Meanwhile, on the waterfront, we were reclaiming the land which was stolen by a storm a few years prior. The erosion was progressively stealing more of the property. Wire baskets were filled with river rocks, which had been brought in by the truckload to build a wall. We were taking a giant step, stretching our arms out wide, believing God for the greater things to come. Little did we know at that time while we were building the wall that it would save us in the future from one of the greatest floods in Guatemala. A year later, in November 2020, Hurricanes Eta and Iota flooded Central America. The wall in the physical realm represents what we will do by faith in the spirit realm. A wall forms protection, making a safe place. Giving a child a safe place promotes freedom. In our case, we strive to bring healing to the hearts of the children—one heart at a time. Again I remind you: God is love, and nothing is impossible with God for those who believe. *Listen, can you hear me*—the Holy Spirit is speaking. Who is listening?

In preparation for making the grounds of Casa Agua Azul beautiful, many rocks had to be placed, replaced, or removed. Our struggles of constant redoing reminded us to count our successes. They also speak spiritual lessons. God constantly communicates to us in our daily lives if only we will listen. Revelation is in the air, for God is alive, speaking in many ways. One day, after the children returned from church activities, they joined forces with us. They are so much fun to work with. Joy is found in creating—through the carrying of rocks, the digging up of rocks, and hauling of concrete blocks. We became one happy family, and before the sun went down, even our neighbor Gerson came over with a shovel in his hand. The sun set, and the sky grew dark, but our hands stayed busy creating because purpose grows the heart and fills the mind with the better things that are yet to come.

It is love which brought me here. The house we prayed for on the shores back in February 2009 spoke. The house cried out, and my mind could see what was not yet, what was beckoning to be born, to be born of the Spirit. It takes a team of dedicated people sold out for what Jesus loves; otherwise, you just might give up. There are times filled with joy and times which are really difficult.

God puts people together. Unity and humility welcome diversity as we walk together with different gifts and talents all given by our Creator to benefit the whole. I am so grateful and overwhelmed by the goodness of God manifested from those who have stepped forth with a heart of love joining forces to help the children.

Rachel, overflowing with love, has been by my side since the beginning. She has the most beautiful eyes, reflecting the beautiful life of her spirit. The depth and richness of her soul is a deep well. I always think of the story of Jacob at the well with his herd. I can't imagine how thirsty those sheep must have been. That is the heart of a true missionary—to lead others to the living water, whether one is leading a sheep, a cow, or a goat to drink. When you look into the eyes of those who thirst, it is only Jesus who can truly satisfy. They are hungry for Jesus, the living water. Rachel is always willing to serve and lead. She is my neighbor in the Florida Keys and the same age as my son. She is instrumental in bringing many teams to the Casa Agua Azul and is an encouragement to her generation.

Like Racheal, Danielle loves to serve on the mission field. It was crazy how I met her. Time has a way of escaping you, but it was many years ago, while in Poptun, Guatemala at Casa Hogar Ahicam. She was leading a mission team from Michigan. I just happened to show up, also with my team, to spend a day with the children. We spoke briefly. I shared with her my vision for another children's home in Ensenada. At that time, we were in the process of purchasing the property. I was heading back to the States, but Danielle still had another week in Guatemala.

On their adventure day, they decided they would go over to the property we were about to purchase, hours away, and pray. Then about a year later, she gave me a call, saying she would like to bring a team to our place. I remembered meeting her, but I really didn't know her, and she didn't know me either. She took a giant leap of faith and showed up in Guatemala City with a team of twelve. We met at the airport with barely a proper introduction. I met her with "Hi, the van just broke down. Follow me." Like I said earlier, *"Let's just get rolling."* Welcome to the mission field.

Christi is one of my greatest advocates and has been my prayer partner ever since we met at a Bible study and found the love of Jesus. Our favorite prayer was "More of the Holy Spirit." At that time, we didn't even know what we were asking for. God has answered, and we continue to pray for more. Christi has been my Aaron and has held my arms up when I haven't been able to find the strength on my own. She's always been there. Christi is a great missionary; we have traveled to Panama, Belize, and the Bahamas together.

My favorite memory is when we were ministering in a little church in Saila, Guatemala. In the beginning of the service, all the people from the village had gathered, and one of our team members became very sick. I went outside with her and another missionary, Joanne. Things became very unusual and dreamlike. The pastor, who was also outside, started prophesying about my life; meanwhile, Mary was getting sick. Joanne, who I call Moo, my personal prayer warrior, was praying over Mary, and that was when I saw Blue Water Surrender and Casa Agua Azul being born. When I walked back into the church, Christi, with a big smile, was leading with song and dance. I knew at that moment that if Christi was with me, I would never have to worry about anything.

Missions are for all ages. We have had missionaries as young as seven and as old as seventy. I challenge you to come at eighty-eight. We'll hike up to the hot waterfalls and jump off the cliff together. That's walking with Jesus. He blindfolds you, leads you down a path, and then he asks you to jump off the cliff. You barely land, and he will ask you to climb up and jump again. Jesus is not boring!

Gaby's perspective is "There is never a dull moment with a missionary." She continued, "As you all may know, my mom is known as Mother Teresa of Guatemala City. I've seen it all. One thing is for sure—when you have a plan, expect the unexpected. As I am here with Gail at Casa Agua Azul, I see the love being poured forth—this is not just a home but a family. My background was similar to the children here. My birth mom passed away when I was nine years old. I lived in a small village with my brother and sisters. After she died, the environment we were living in was unsafe. That's when this missionary couple took us in and loved us. Then there was another unfortunate event. We were struggling. My missionary mom showed me with her actions how to handle life when it gets tough. She placed the love of God and faith in my heart. This is what I want to pass on to the children and others. It changed my life, and it can change theirs. I encourage you to share your life with someone less fortunate. We all have something to give. We all are loved and valued by Jesus."

A TRAIL OF THE HOLY SPIRIT

Gaby has been a blessing by my side for my entire journey since I met her years ago. She has shared joy, wisdom, and encouragement. When I have felt hopeless, her big beautiful smile has lifted me on high. We have laughed many a time in the good times and the bad as life is a full circle.

Having a great relationship with the people of Ensenada is vital to our success. The village is small and remote, and people live very close to the earth. Farming is their main means of support—whether for money or purely to provide food for the family. Chickens run free, and so do the pigs! Children play on the street, and the dogs lie down in the middle of the road, oblivious to a car passing by. You really need to be careful when you drive in the village. We found this out the hard way one fall season. A great team had sailed in from Florida aboard sailing vessel *Adonai*. Captain Josh and Jamie brought in an alumni World Race group. We had hosted three World Race teams in the past and were ecstatic to have this one. World Race is a wonderful ten-month program where teams of young adults visit eleven countries and come alongside small ministries to be the hands and feet of Jesus.

Captain Josh was innocently driving in the village with his group in the back of the truck. Right before he turned the corner to Casa Agua Azul, a very unfortunate incident took place. Josh ran over and killed the prize goose of a neighboring house. Of course, it was owned by the villager who was already upset with us. When you hit an animal in a village, you own it. With an American killing the goose, it became a very expensive goose and an opportunity for Jerry to smooth things over. On a very serious note, in a neighboring village, a truck accidentally hit a child, and the truck driver literally was pulled out of the truck, had gasoline poured on him, and was torched. When you're in the outer regions, it is not uncommon for the law to be taken into the hands of the villagers. Though I am not in agreement with this practice, it is the way it is. Thankfully, I consider Guatemala and our village safe despite the occasional uproar, which is usually for a valid reason. It's a different culture and a different mindset, and they love their children.

Working as a missionary here in Guatemala has really changed my view on many things. We Americans come from an intensely different culture compared to the majority of the world. We are unique in ourselves. The majority in our country live in a society with advanced technology, education, and science. We have a prosperous free market with money placed at our fingertips for anyone who really wants to work. People flood our borders thinking that if they can get to America, then everything will be fine; it's as if they will win the lottery. Guatemala, in its modern city life, is bustling and going strong while the countryside is filled with natural resources; wonderful, warm, friendly people living in an abundance of beauty. I am able to see that every culture has its complications. I cannot say one is better than the other. We all are able to learn from each other. God is the superior one; we are all his children.

Guatemala has been an eye-opening journey, far outside of my safe American box. Extending a hand to others is our mission; along the way, we love to explore and play on a "Jerry Jungle Tour," seeing life like a local. It is exhilarating to climb a mountain and discover a hidden waterfall or jump into a river within an underground cave only to look up and see a viper. Our teams love to travel to Livingston, located at the mouth of the Rio Dulce. It is home to the Garifuna, another culture present in Guatemala. Jerry is our director of Casa Agua Azul and was born in Guatemala but moved to the United States as an adolescent. He served in the US Marines and returned to his homeland, where he met beautiful Griselda, and is now the father to the children at Casa Agua Azul. He is a man of the jungle. He will cut off the head of a poisonous snake before you even knew it was there. He climbs the mountain like a billy goat while you're standing there panting, sweating, and waiting for your heart rate to slow down. The mountains are hot and steep with beauty hidden amid the jungle, a treasure beyond belief. The love of discovering new waterfalls and making friends in remote villages is beyond words; the wilderness and the way of life are astounding. The perspective of an innocent Guatemala City girl on a mission was that the snakes in the city are just in the zoo. Little did she know she was going to hold a six-foot-long bright-green viper and pose for a photo.

If you haven't taken an overseas mission trip outside of the USA, you will eventually have to go, or else you will never go. "Cross

Fit Ali" was just that. Not only is she strong, but she is brave. Rachel had shared a lot of mission experiences with Ali, and Ali decided she wanted to join our team. Due to her work schedule, her flight didn't match up with the rest of the team members. I really don't like people flying into Guatemala on their own. I like them to be with a group. In this case, because Gaby's mom, Riechelle, was willing to pick her up at the airport, we made an exception. Ali was about to hit the ground and get rolling like never before. Riechelle picked Ali up and brought her to the dump ministry in Guatemala City, where she teaches English to the children who live in the dump. Then they met our private driver, Luis, at Cemaco, a hardware store on the outskirts of Guatemala City. When they arrived in Ensenada, where Casa Agua Azul is located, without a breath, we said, "Hi Ali! Follow us. We need you to take some photos of the pig's private areas to relay a message." We were all laughing so hard. It was one of those moments in life where you cannot contain yourself. Laughter is good medicine! Ali jumped in like a trooper. We were documenting the problem of pigs spreading disease to the children by the "gifts" they leave in the street. That was Ali's baptism in the stream of "let's get rolling" in Guatemala.

Sometimes you may wonder what the heck you are doing not knowing how to approach a situation. There are many things that threaten to harm the children. I believe trying something even if it's out of the ordinary is better than turning your face and pretending everything is okay. Pig manure in the streets is causing many children to become sick and is a big problem as the free range pigs are part of the culture. I don't believe in renovating someone's culture, but I do want to stop those suffering within it.

Missionaries often have to think fast when their faith is tested and the pressure is on. A common situation is when your checked bags are overweight. You find yourself at check-in with a dilemma. More so, it's the line behind you! This will cause a hurried restuffing. Certain airlines are more restrictive than others, and they all have their own set of rules, which, consequently, can become costly. When you are going on a mission trip, people are very generous to donate items. Getting the items to the destination becomes an art. Finding the way is the challenge and worth the smiles from those who will finally receive the items.

Enthusiastic leaders bring forth supercharged whirlwind mission trips, and Danielle is one of those leaders. She is inspiring, full of endless energy, and excited to serve. On one of her trips, complications found her with fifty excess pounds of donations to go into her three already-stuffed suitcases, but somehow, this wonderful team made it to the airport in the US loaded to the gills and cleared customs. The twelve people with twelve jam-packed suitcases and sixteen backpacks was a small amount compared to the nine women in the jungle who had 1,200 pounds of luggage! Needless to say, this did become a challenge for our driver in Guatemala! I was praying that once all was stacked on top of the van, it would remain there. We have had a mishap in the past, losing a suitcase or two; and then if it rains, it becomes even more fun.

As I said before, missionaries may find themselves in a dilemma and have to think quickly. The items they carry, donated from friends who want to help, become blessings to many. Outside of our children's home, we like to bring aid to the schools because education will change the future for these children. Danielle, being a teacher, always prepares a lesson to empower the children and to share the Gospel. In spite of all these complications at the beginning of their trip, her team accomplished a successful mission. Teaching at the local school, they presented the value of taking care of the earth and being good stewards of what God has given us. The team poured out endless love to the children. They were able to explore a remote village, experiencing God in new ways, personally growing their faith, all the while giving their hands in service to Casa Agua Azul and our village. God truly does go before us. It is a choice to trust him—often despite our feelings. God is exciting as he shows up in personal ways.

There is joy in serving others, but sometimes it propels you into awkward situations. Your comfort level will be tested to stand against many situations that have the element of surprise. Your energy and physical strength will be pushed, your emotions will waver, but your heart will be touched, and you will find joy in the journey as you grow and take victory in your own life and in the lives of others. I believe this is the essence of missions. Competition has no place of honor. Humility is what wins and stands exalted in the end, for this is where the glory of God shines. Sweet surrender to rely on God is what will make you soar higher.

On this particular trip with Danielle's supercharged group, we had an impromptu opportunity to serve in Rio Bonito, a remote village off a tributary of the Rio Dulce. It is only in recent years, the early 2000s, that missionaries have traveled there. The first man who arrived in this village was a tall gentleman from Texas named Phil. As Jerry tells the story, the village chief had all the children in his hut, hiding, believing the White man was coming with ill intention. The village had not yet been exposed to the outside world. However, today, because of the passion of this missionary, higher education is taught in the village through Titus International Missions. I don't know how Phil was able to gain their trust, but I know that Jerry had a hand in that situation. Jerry has a way of resolving tensions with good-natured humor; he somehow managed to convince them that Phil was not going to harm the children; thus, a ministry was born.

As a result of this man's work and Jerry's heart, I was blessed to become the leader of the second mission group to go into the village and visit the school. The Gospel of Jesus was new to them, and I remember our first visit. There were four of us. On the spur of the moment, we decided to take a mission adventure with the extra donated school supplies we had carried from the United States. First, we loaded up in Jerry's jeep. After passing through town, we headed off down the unbeaten path, which was a bumpy, dusty road though the jungle. After forty minutes or so, we suddenly stopped and got out in a cow pasture. A red dirt path was ahead. The sun was beating down on us as we hiked, carrying heavy packs of supplies, passing cows along the way.

Eventually, we arrived at a stream. After crossing the knee-deep stream, there was a new path through a banana field which was winding past a few reed huts. After climbing through some barbed wire, we reached the center of the village then proceeded to the school. We were met by the principal, other village residents, and a group of children. By organizing games and playing duck, duck goose, and jump rope, we were able to break the ice; then we painted with the children while sharing about Jesus and ended by praying for them. Before we left, we signed an official book, recording our visit and the supplies we had given. We were some of the first missionaries to come and serve in the village.

We love to extend our hand, come alongside, and be of service and join God where he is working. We were trusted to go into a family's hut, which was essentially a hollow living space. A small area was set apart for a one pot fire for cooking. The rest of the house was empty. I do not remember their names, but I do remember that I was struck by the quietness and simplicity of their lives. It caused me to wonder about them. What do they think and dream about? Are they happy? It was a mystery and left me with many questions in my heart about the different realities we live in. I remember as a child being happy in a tree house, but as an adult, my mind is so busy; would I be able to live in such simplicity again? Would my mind ever find peace? As they looked at us, they too had a pondering wonder on their faces.

Since that time, many others have come including Danielle's Michigan team; one particular mission trip, on another spontaneous adventure to Rio Bonita, we first stopped over at Boatique to drop some supplies for our missionary friends Pamela and Sheldon. I had met Pamela on the phone while in the Florida Keys! In 2018, they were sailing on their boat and arrived in Key Largo, Florida, where Pamela felt moved to go to a church service near the marina they were staying at! The pastor made an announcement—which he almost had forgotten—at the end of the church service for our annual benefit for Casa Agua Azul. That is when she called me to buy tickets. We spoke briefly and found out that we both had husbands who liked flying and sailing, loved Jesus, and had roots in Texas. I was certain I wanted to meet this couple at our event. We became instant friends, and they decided to make Guatemala their next sailing adventure stop. Arriving in Guatemala, they volunteered at Casa Agua Azul, blessing us in numerous ways, and we attribute the building of the director's house to their hands and heart. While serving, they fell in love with Guatemala, bringing back memories of time past especially for Sheldon. They became missionaries to Guatemala and developed

Boatique Hotel, a tucked-away gem in the monkey preserve of the Rio Dulce. We are all here to help each other, and when we join together, greater things are sure to come!

After our stop at Boatique, Danielle's team continued in enthusiasm for what was ahead. It was a stifling, hot, full day as we continued traveling down the river. The oppressive heat was melting us like ice cream in the sun; you could drink our gallons of salty sweat. Then in a moment, the sky was overcast, allowing a breath of relief for a split second. Heat is the price you pay to explore the many concealed treasures which are at every twist of the river. Navigating off the river, we slowly passed through a reed-covered entrance to the tributary, avoiding the hidden tree stumps, to find Rio Bonito. Following the tributary deeper into the mountainous region, we eventually tied up to a root on the riverbank. The river happened to be high due to much rain.

As we stepped out of the boat, we found ourselves surrendering to the mud, often knee deep. We trudged the path, some happy and some bewildered with mud-soaked tennis shoes. The cows occasionally looked up with a wondering "moo." Finally, in sight was the soccer field filled with the village children, and any woe was now turned to excitement. John, a team member with a soccer ball in hand, and the rest of us with bubbles and a Frisbee had an instant connection! After an afternoon of running in the hot sun, our team prayed for the children and shared God's wisdom and love.

We love to pack action and fun into our trips. After leaving Rio Bonito, there was an opportunity to go "lily pad" shopping. This is where the locals come out on the river in *cayucos* and share their wares. It's a local floating market of handmade jewelry, carvings, and beautiful local crafts. Afterward, we were all ready for more adventure. We explored the sulfur springs which pour out of the rock crevices beneath the surface along the shores of the Rio Dulce. Then we ventured into the caves on the hillside above.

We wrapped up the day exploring the grounds of Camp Rio Dulce, which serves over three hundred children of the region, sharing the love of Christ with them every January. It is a combined effort of Titus Ministry and Camp Compass, both ministries birthed in the heart of Texas. There are so many people working together to advance the kingdom of God in wonderful creative ways. I see an outpouring of passion unique to each individual heart—all of which has great value.

If you don't pay attention, one day turns into the next when activity is fast paced. It becomes a whirlwind of events. Our work is spiritual and physical at the same time—you never know what will happen next. I have never met such diverse groups of people in one place, working toward a similar goal. We welcome volunteers from every walk of life, and our work changes constantly with the needs of the people we serve. For example, we have been building a retaining wall to hold back the lake from eroding the property. At the time of this writing, two more loads of rocks were close to being gone, all carried by hand to be placed in wire baskets, making a barrier. Construction is but one of the many tasks we perform in Jesus's name.

To bless our village of Ensenada in a healthy way, we host yard sales. The yard sale is in front of our gate on the street. We set out tables and place our goods on them, which are sold for one quetzal or so, which is basically for pennies. This allows everyone to be able to purchase what they need, then we bless the local church with the leftover items and some of the yard sale proceeds.

Giving is important, but we also do not want to breed expectations and become a handout mission. This will only bring momentary joy, thinking you have helped where possibly you have not. This does not rule out the person who is in dire straits or severely in need. It is important to pray and seek God's direction. Your actions affect those who remain on the mission field and those who will come after you. We often learn through our own mistakes and the mistakes of others to avoid as many pitfalls as possible. We have learned from other missionaries a great way to bless others is by hosting games and contests, using gifts as prizes, which will avoid the pitfall of handouts and expectations.

One particular short-term missionary stands out to me as I look back on my history with Guatemala. It was Danielle's son Carter. I met him when he was nine years old and came on a mission trip. We were going to have a meeting, so I asked him to sit with Gabriella, a young girl who was drawing and taking notes. I gave him a pencil also to take notes with and to just hang out. To my surprise, God came over him, and he started to draw prophetically. He was really touched by God.

On this trip, he insisted on being baptized despite being away from his home church and many family members to witness such a great decision. We baptized him at the most beautiful waterfalls before he went home. He went home speaking forth truth and evangelizing on the airplane. A passenger on the plane gave him his first dollar to start his ministry. He now paints with a heart of love, giving words of knowledge, leaving behind his mark of incredible pure love.

Some of our missionaries' focus is also aimed at building up our local staff. The local staff carries a large burden at times due to the nature of our work with vulnerable children. Everyone has personal experiences in their lives which are of value to build others up. I like to keep my mind open to the ideas of others, and I find there is always something new to learn. Staying connected and united in thought brings forth our best efforts. I encourage you to share your experience and bring your wisdom and talent forward. Children are the next generation of future leaders. Your testimony has the ability to bring strength and hope to those who come into your path.

Pouring into the children of the village is a priority of Blue Water Surrender, and mission teams do this oh so well. An important part of any mission is to partner with your local leaders such as those from the church and school. This will help you achieve overall success, and it shows respect. We reach out to the children through biblical song, dance, games, and art to inspire our neighbors to love God. The children are the driving force to change. For instance, community cleanup is a countercultural concept. We were so excited when close to a hundred children, joined by parents, went into the community, picking up trash! Our truck was piled high with bags and bags of trash—a great start to our mission. The group was so enthusiastic they went into home trash cans to add to the delivery we were soon to make. Our main focus was to share the Gospel by being good stewards of the planet that God gave to us. Stewardship is showing a grateful heart to the Lord; part of that stewardship involves cultivating the environment for good health and wellbeing. The planet takes care of us, so we need to take care of the planet.

We made many trips to the landfill to discard the trash bags. There is no trash pickup service in our village. Often trash is burned, releasing toxic plastics in the air. Trash is also simply tossed aside. Awareness is the beginning of change. Like any other skill, sanitation has to be practiced; it is a constant topic. The community is good at repurposing and recycling, but the mindset on trash is an ongoing challenge. It will not change overnight. We are working with the children—the hope is education of the next generation as adults are often resistant to change no matter where you are.

We like to work, and we like to play! Our mission teams love to walk the trail just a couple of miles up the way to visit the hot waterfalls. Two rivers meet, sending steam into the air where the icy cold blends with the hot spring, pouring over the stacked-high rocks in the mountains. It is the perfect way to end a hot and sweaty day, many times with the surprise of a baptism.

Lighting a campfire on the shores of Lake Izabal to share s'mores with the children of Casa Agua Azul is fun. Popping popcorn in the kitchen adds delight to the day. As you take the time to read a book or place a puzzle together, it may be the very first time for some of our children. These special moments are life-giving and healing while the mending of hearts is taking place in bruised lives.

In general, it is important to rest because work is never finished. Many decisions are endlessly filled with details. Pipes, sinks, toilets, and drain fields are necessary to house children. Many experiences teach you that once built, they will only need to be repaired, so build strong. Guatemala has the most beautiful hardwoods to work with. I find relief from the stress of building by thinking about furniture and what we are able to build with our collection of wood that will be fun and functional. I love creating furniture and objects from them. It's important to keep a balance and have fun to keep the joy in serving.

I have found the greatest work is to pray. It is powerful to pray with others who have a prayerful heart and pound on heaven's door to intercede for the children. Prayer is powerful: it opens and closes doors and will change your life. Honesty of heart avails much. God's word does not come back void. Many times the situation may not change, but peace has a way of entering your heart. One of my prayers took years to be answered, but it was *answered*. At first, it was acceptance of things as they are. God answers in his time, so keep in mind "patient endurance."

Our main structure on the property has many flaws since it is an old remodeled jungle building constructed from wood, which shrinks and swells with the weather. There is endless, tedious attention needed at every turn. It can only be repaired with a labor of love. My answer to this prayer was Brandon from Texas. Month after month, he worked with his hands, sealed up cracks, repaired wire, pipe, windows, and what seemed like a gazillion more things. The faithfulness of God is worth waiting for, and I am so grateful to receive it.

When you come to Casa Agua Azul, you become part of our family. To watch our staff load up and squeeze into our two vehicles with eighteen children or more, you may have mixed feelings. It is not uncommon in Guatemala to see an entire family of four on a small motor bike without helmets or a woman riding side saddle with a baby on her lap as they speed down the road at fifty miles per hour. One of our visiting missionaries was so touched by one family's plight she bought a truck for the family so they would be able to transport the mother, who was suffering with a chronic illness, safely to the hospital.

The Guatemalan mode of transportation differs greatly from downtown USA. In Guatemala, as discussed, you see families squeezed on to small motorcycles, but it is also common to see a pickup truck with sixteen or more crammed in the back.

The open market in El Estor is vibrant and full of color. It is so refreshing to take some free time and immerse yourself into the local culture and to shop for authentic souvenirs. Locals bring an abundance of vegetables to sell while people wander about in their everyday lives. To an American, it is exciting as life is so different here. I have found this culture to be refreshing and kind, with relationships being highly valued. People are relaxed, living in the moment, allowing for the unexpected to break into the day, giving surprise and wonder. You see God's hand at work all around you. These unplanned, unexpected moments become your greatest treasures.

One of my favorite team trips was to visit and explore the nature preserve of Seacacar. As I was hiking with a group and some preteen missionaries, to our surprise, tucked in the rocks was a hidden coral snake and iridescent colored beetles the size of walnuts. To add to our already-raised heartbeat, we were confronted with intense heat as we faced the steep climb to the top of the cliff. The reward was overlooking the river canyon some eight hundred feet below. Next was a Mayan cave located along the path which runs above the river. The view and nature's fresh air will revive your soul time and time again. The trail often has howler monkeys in the treetops, making a racket drowning out the songs of the birds. The jungle is filled with butterflies dancing above exotic plants and flowers.

At the end of the trail, a home-cooked Mayan meal is prepared and served for you accompanied with cold drinks! Fully refreshed, we found the way back down is much easier and fun. It is as if you are in an adventure movie scene as you float down the cool river in tubes to pass through the eight-hundred-foot canyon walls. Looking up in silence, I could hear the captivating, thrilling sounds native to the area. Echoing against the cliff into your soul, the bliss of God's creation penetrates my heart every time. At the end of the trail, I never want to leave the peace I have found.

I feel sad when teams leave as what we have experienced together becomes a bonding of spirits. Deep places that we often don't know existed have been touched, creating a longing for more. God is everywhere, and what our heart longs for will never leave us. Our heart is like a treasure chest. In order to receive, it must be open; and in order to give, it must remain open. The age-old saying is true: If you want to keep what you have, then you will give it away. After a trip, we love to share stories with others, stay in contact with each other, and dream of days to come when we will be united once again.

Jesus says, "Truly, I tell you, whatever you did for one of the least of these brothers and sisters of mine, you did for me" (Matthew 25:40). There are people hurting all over the world, in our neighborhoods, and even in our own homes. Compassion and love will fuel any mission. God places a certain region on each person's heart—be it Brazil, Guatemala, Mexico or just across the street. We are all called to help our brothers and sisters anywhere and everywhere, most importantly, to come into relationship with God.

The love for children has attracted many to Casa Agua Azul. Love is of high value and has been the healing agent, a priority to the people who have come and served. Many short-term mission teams have poured out their hearts through their hands, building and doing activities with the children. Others have stayed for extended periods of time, making deeper relationships with the children. Each person has left their mark by touching the life of another, and in return, they have been touched themselves by God, the source of healing and love. No matter the background or circumstances of a person, just like the children, we all need a touch from heaven. Our mission has prevailed through faith, which never fails when we base our faith on truth. We are grateful to those who have come and put their hands to the plow, sharing their gifts and talents, remembering the greatest gift you have is love. What you do matters because love never fails.

Man is made in the image of God to be his beloved child. My prayer is that mankind will possess the eyes of God and use his hands to bring many blessings to all the children in the world.

> They will be like a tree planted by the water that sends out its roots by the stream. It does not fear when heat comes; its leaves are always green. It has no worries in a year of drought and never fails to bear fruit. (Jeremiah 17:8 NIV)

Loved poured forth

8

Victory, Defiance, and Darkness

With the Coronavirus continuing around the world, my stay at Casa Agua Azul was extended. At this time, I was able to witness some of the adverse ways in which our children behave. Each child has lived in abusive situations. Much of their behavior comes from a place of pain, and they act out accordingly.

When a child sprays bleach on all the clean laundry of his three bunk mates, but not his own, claiming it's an accident, you have to shake your head and wonder. We had been praying earlier that day for wisdom about keeping the children safe from the virus. Now it was time to pray for wisdom and discernment for a solution to avoid further harm to our child acting out. Prayer is our first best action to take. These children are not like their peers who grow up in loving homes. Being angry will not solve anything. Giving grace, with accountability, is what is needed.

Defiance is not a stranger. It is a repeated behavior manifesting from a few of our children in the house. One specific child, who has the greatest smile and a kind heart, is constantly acting in defiance. It wears our staff down, resulting in many moments of difficulty and frustration. The children come from many different backgrounds, and their stories vary, but the one thing that they have in common is pain—unresolved pain, which manifests in their behaviors and actions, which baffles you. The authorities arrived one time for a surprise inspection. One of our children was up in the tree as they drove in, and he decided to urinate on them from his lofty perch. A sense of humor will help you not lose your mind or be embarrassed beyond words in such a situation. We have a professional staff working with the children on a regular basis. To rebuild a life is a constant process which takes an entire team to be in agreement and participate. It is rare that a day goes by without conflict.

We spend many hours sitting at the table overlooking Lake Izabal, contemplating and looking for solutions. It's a place for our staff to come together to defuse so they can power back up to be poured out again. The children need love. The holes in their hearts are huge. It is vital to come from a place of love in your heart to be able to help them in their struggles. Without love, we will only be a clanging gong causing more harm (1 Corinthians 13:1). The best teacher is you modeling patience and love with healthy boundaries. Their boundaries have been broken by the ones who were supposed to love and protect them the most. A compassionate heart is necessary not only for the children but for their family and parents. You will need to think about what must have happened to them to become this way. Hurt people hurt people. Hurt needs healing, and no one on the planet is exempt. Some have greater hurt than others. May compassion and empathy rule in our hearts to love without conditions.

Justice likes to speak loudly. What about justice? To judge another will only cause more pain; it is better to listen with an empathic ear than to place judgment on another human being. A wise person knows their place, and justice belongs to God—in his time. We are not the judge.

Honesty and integrity are qualities that bond and bind trust. Looking deep into the spirit will reveal the intention of the heart. We are human, and all make mistakes. This is where grace is to abound. Situations will arise, and how you respond is critical. Our response will either place us in a prison of our own making, or we will walk away free. To be aware that you have this choice is empowering. How often do we react on our preprogrammed autopilot? We are not even aware of our own reaction, blind to ourselves. I suppose we all have a skeleton or two in the closet, yet we do not have to live blind. There is freedom. Freedom came with a price, and freedom comes with a responsibility to be walked out by each individual. Do you know your worth to the Creator of the universe, the one who created you and loves you forever unconditionally?

While remodeling the physical safe house and laying the necessary groundwork to be a legal entity, I was met with a big challenge; I was in a very vulnerable place in my spirit. A person close and dear to my heart revealed something about their current life which would have an effect on the future plans of Casa Agua Azul. Even under ordinary circumstances, this would have been difficult to digest and work through, but I believe in finding solutions to complicated situations. The timing, however, placed the situation into a totally different light. I was shocked and not able to say much, but I swallowed hard and began to process the new information. The next day, while still dazed, another bomb was dropped into my arms. You want to talk about being in an awkward situation? This was one of them.

Innocence looks you in the face, and what are you to do? I too am human, with emotions and a mind that seriously needs to process and pray. In relationships, I believe honesty and integrity are the basis of trust, and they are of high value. When one hides the truth for a year, trust is broken. At the same time, it is a very brave soul to come forth and reveal a hidden truth especially when they know it is against a certain belief. I respect the boldness taken here. In this case, the situation goes against core beliefs of our organization and what Casa Agua Azul stands for and represents.

In life, it is best to tell the truth up front; waiting only delays and increases inevitable pain. I felt betrayed and manipulated and my heart was absolutely broken. I was shocked by the hiding. Trust is a two-way street. I can only imagine that that individual may not have trusted my character as a leader to make a good decision. My eyes are fixed on the potential of what lies within each person, the hope for which they are called. I firmly believe there is a calling on each person's life. God has created each person for a good purpose. If you have faith in the goodness of God, you must also believe in the evil opponent of God. Darkness is relentless, but the love of God is greater. This is where our help comes from.

God was about to do a mighty work in my heart. I was not the same after that betrayal; it was a long hard road for my heart to recover. My mind was unable to focus for over a year. I am not proud to share my brokenness, but at the same time, I lay down my pride to expose it. Life has its lessons—this was a big one; it happened just prior to my mother's ninety-first birthday and a huge family party. My body was present, but that was all. My mind and spirit were in darkness. I felt no joy at the celebration of someone I loved so dearly. Without hesitation, darkness had taken me captive. I was able to extend my hand in forgiveness and grace, but the hurt and the pain started to run, rule, and reign.

In this place of hurt, I had to habitually pay attention to my thoughts. If I am not careful, my thoughts will try to wander into a dark and dangerous place, thinking I know why someone acted a certain way. No one is able to know the mind of another, only God. The truth is that unless a person tells you why, you do not know. You do not want your heart to become hard with judgment. Instead, lean into understanding, where compassion has a way of softening the heart. I am to look and see where my own motive lies and realize we all have different reasons for what we do. It is important to think the best of others, then the hurt and pain will be shortened.

We are not to fight alone. God is with us, and so is wise counsel and the Word of God. I was learning to walk in new truths. Difficult decisions were ahead—ones that would alter the long-awaited and joyfully anticipated future of one you love so deeply and had great vision for. Emotions on both sides suffered an assault. Decisions are not to be made from emotion or pain. They are to be made with a heart settled in love right before God, not according to self. It is a choice to make if you will trust God or not.

"Trust in God" is easier said than done. Have you ever struggled with trust? We all struggle to trust others, and we also struggle to trust God; but truly, God is the one we can trust. God never changes; his nature is love. God is just, and he is love. He is above all things and loves his creation of man so greatly that he made us in his image.

I had to get my heart right, which took a couple of months. I did not desire to speak from my flesh with my now slightly distanced friend. We had continued to communicate over other matters at hand but never addressed the solution to our mutual challenge. It was important that this was not a mere difference in cultures. I spoke with two local pastors, looking for wisdom to be certain we would not be outside the culture of Guatemala. I also went for counsel with my pastor in the United States. I believe it is important to make fair decisions not only for myself but for all concerned, so I listened to different perspectives and both sides of a story. Regardless of how we try to avoid conflict, life happens and harm occurs, but a way to navigate out was ahead. There is nothing new that God has not seen before. The Word of God is our best guide; it never fails, and neither does the voice of the Holy Spirit.

I had my own fears to face, which is not easy, but it leads to freedom every time. Facing fear confronts our trust in God. We question, is God for us? Is he greater? The what-ifs start to rally; their goal is to stop you. The mountain of fear you are facing is surrounded by a dark storm which is all just a facade, attempting to hide a big fat lie cleverly disguised. We need to push past all of that and grab hold of trust and truth. You were made to be a mountain mover and an earth shaker. God is greater. He is the greatest of all. His heart is love—unconditional love for all.

It was obvious the hand of God was parting our ways. It was time to let go and trust God to fulfill each of our destinies. God's plan does not leave a place void. God is trustworthy and true to his word. He sent new people to walk by my side and new people to walk by my old friend's side. He will do the same for you.

There have been many trials and tribulations along the way including mission trips where Satan has gotten a foothold; this is when sifting takes place. Emotional triggers escalate and quarrels arise; hurt feelings are the rotten fruit of such trees. Walls of protection start to build, and defensiveness turns friends into opponents. Intentions may be right and pure, but once the deceiver has dug his claws in, a battle has started. Prayer and the passage of time are the way out.

In the waiting, if you allow, God is working. We can only change ourselves, not others. Our action or our reaction opened a door, and that door needs to be closed. Inviting God to reveal which thoughts are out of alignment with his truth reveals our method of operation. The motive in our heart may be misguided and in need of correction. God disciplines those he loves, and the wise will heed the Spirit of God at work. Our hearts are in need of healing, and our minds need to come into the truth. It is a human condition where pride can halt the process of reconciliation within ourselves first.

To reconcile a relationship, it takes two, and when peace and healing come, a once-strained friendship is stronger than before. Iron has sharpened iron. The process of sanctification, which takes a lifetime, is at hand. We have this gift through forgiveness and repentance by faith. To turn to God in all matters is a blessed life. God is with us in the fire.

With everything in life, there are two sides to every coin. Our perspectives vary depending on our life experiences, what we have been taught and have learned along the way. We don't know what others have gone through in life, and they will not know what you have gone through either. Good communication is key. It takes willingness to listen—people want to be heard and understood. It is a skill to be developed along with our words as we speak. When a storm arises, steering the ship away from the rocks of destruction comes from a steady hand on the tiller; so it is with our tongue.

Darkness is on the planet, roaming. We see it everywhere, and it appears to be increasing at an alarming rate. Protesters in Guatemala erecting roadblocks are as common as peanut butter and jelly. Many protests you come upon are a surprise while others are scheduled and advertised. Most protests are peaceful, but not all. On more than one occasion, the Guatemala military has been called in to keep peace in our area. This is when a boat comes in handy to go by way of the water to and from town. Flexibility and patience are required; there have been countless times when for days we have not been able to travel past certain points. It is stressful when you are trying to make a flight in Guatemala City. Even leaving a day ahead is not foolproof. One time, we had to arrive at the airport at 5:00 a.m. for a 1:00 p.m. flight. We are determined to find a way with patience, endurance, and adaptation.

A TRAIL OF THE HOLY SPIRIT

Life in the jungle is different. Disease comes in different forms. Insects, snakes, food, and water affect our health. Some of our visitors have digestive discomfort, but it is not always because of uncleanliness. Different bacteria which are present in this part of the world will cause our systems to react just as a foreigner in the USA may experience. I call this type of discomfort the Guatemala crud. There is another illness that strikes people down. Amoebas present in the environment can contaminate food, water, or your hands, making you very ill. A trip to the clinic and a handful of antibiotics is the sure cure. I have had this experience twice. It is not fun, but you will live.

Witchcraft and witch doctors practice their faith openly here. I have been awakened with intense dreams and the feelings of darkness pressing on my soul. I remember being startled one night from a deep sleep with the vision of a house and the word *witchcraft* being whispered while the most excruciating pain came over my body. I prayed and prayed to make it through the night. In the morning, faithful Luis came and carried me to the clinic. I had a UTI, but the doctor was confused as I was on medication for an amoeba, so he did not think it possible for such an infection to occur under the circumstances. Some things just happen and are a mystery, and they will remain a mystery; that is not the only time strange, intense pain has appeared and struck me down.

Pain has a way of coming on suddenly. Death is no stranger, and it alters lives at the snap of the finger. I witnessed a miracle seeing baby Kimberly so close to death. She was gray in color, and I watched her come to life, looking into her mother's eyes, bonding in love, one of the most joyful moments on the mission field—only to die a couple of months later. One of the hardest things I ever had to do was send money for a casket and for the funeral. In US culture, death is wrapped fairly clean. I will never forget walking into a hut in our village with a family wailing. The man was in the hammock, surrounded by his wife and children. He was so ill; death was knocking on the door. We prayed for him and were able to help him get scheduled for surgery with a medical mission group coming soon. Unfortunately, he was not able to hold on to life long enough to make the surgery. This was so sad. These moments stay with you deep in your heart.

When death hits close to home and takes the spouse of one of your Guatemalan team members at a young age, grief runs deep. The hopes and dreams you had with this person vanished, then a vacancy in your heart remains. I learned in our village that when a person dies, it is customary for each household to pitch in a bag of cement, rebar, or cinder blocks to aid in the burial process, which is done by hand, upfront and personal. Death is part of life, and eventually, we have to come to terms with it.

The human race is suffering. Presidential elections in the United States, most recently with Trump and Biden, are triggering a great division, with riots causing great harm to many innocent people. Disagreement on a national level is a mindset. A spirit of darkness is moving in. Many have been shot in Guatemala during election periods. It is dangerous to be a politician. Lives are being lost because others have a different opinion. What we do and what we speak matters. Do we want war, or do we want peace?

Kindness counts. A friend of mine, Amy, who is a teacher, desires to share love and peace to stand against the causes of war, which starts at a young age. She teaches the "five Cs" to be a better student or a better person in anything you do: consciousness, compassion, communication, cooperation, and composure. This is a great lesson. We can all learn to stand against the things that cause us to stumble or not live the abundant, loving life God calls us to live.

I often will have to question myself, *Where is my faith in the moment?* With misdirected faith, my life at one time was trapped in darkness; the evidence was all around me. I was hurting others and myself. No one is exempt from this condition. We are human, and we err. The saying "there but for the grace of God go I" is the basis to form a foundation of compassion. Compassion ruling in a heart is a powerful weapon against darkness.

Today my life is different because my faith does not rest in myself but in God. Where we place our faith in life affects the results of our life and reflects the amount of peace and joy we will walk in. With God, all things are possible.

At many times, we have to push past what is attempting to stop us. I have traveled to Guatemala in a wheelchair with my shin skinned down to the bone. I had to put aside the fear of infection to pursue what was ahead. If I stopped when I was ill, I may never leave the United States. There is always something adverse to deal with in life.

God promises to never leave us nor to forsake us. This does not mean a trouble-free life. It is a false belief if you think that you will never have trouble when you turn your life over to God. Jesus has said,

> I have told you these things, so that in me you may have peace. In this world you will have trouble. But take heart! I have overcome the world. (John 16:33 NIV)

Love has been freely given on the cross for a purpose. Our freedom from darkness is the victory won at the cross. True freedom came with a price. Jesus, before he took his last breath, said, "It is finished." The word *finished* means "complete"; nothing more needs to be added. The darkness of sin has been put to death once and for all. There is a war against our souls. It is clear to see. Just look around—there is pain and suffering in the world. The beauty of a loving, just God is that he gives each person a choice to make. This is the basis of freedom. Because of freedom and free will in our world today, pain and suffering continue to grow. I have a choice to make with every breath I take. Will I remain in darkness and partake in pain and suffering from wrongdoings?

This world no longer has absolutes, causing confusion and chaos, a made up world of what pleases man. There is another world, a kingdom, filled with grace and mercy which was based on the law, which distinguishes a right from a wrong. One day, there will be no more pain and suffering for those who are in the kingdom. Until then, there is a purpose for our life as well as a plan. I believe this, and my life testifies this is true. The plan—God's plan is to believe. John 3:16 states it clearly: God gave his only son, and whoever will believe in him will have eternal life. It is a choice to believe or not. There is a gift to be received, and it is by faith. There is an Author to this faith, who is a person who comes to us in spirit and truth, a mystery which unfolds and reveals more. Here nothing in your life will ever be wasted.

The Author makes all things work together for the good, the benefit of those who love him. God's kingdom is advancing and going forth. That is why we are here. He desires for what he created to return to its true nature. We are his workmanship, created in love. Because he makes all things work together for the good of those who love him, our lives are about personal transformation. It is not about achieving a goal; it's about how we achieve the goal. In our lives, we are here to reflect the light of Jesus Christ. It is his life which he freely gave at the cross to give us life everlasting, to the full.

A new day Casa Agua Azul

9

Don't Fight the River

As life goes on, "fighting the river" will only exhaust you! We are into the second week of the Coronavirus. Today Jerry will drive Gaby at 5:00 a.m. halfway to Guatemala City. Her family will meet them there because of curfew. I will miss her and having someone to talk to in English. Jerry is bilingual, but aside from him, I will be on my own. You would think after all these years, I would have a grip on the Spanish language, but it just does not come to me naturally. More *Duolingo* is in order!

I may not like the flow of the river at the moment. My question is, *Can I change it?* The US State Department charter flights are starting to evacuate Americans from Guatemala. I applied for a flight but days later have not heard anything back. A 4:00 p.m., curfew is now being mandated in Guatemala, with strict enforcement. This morning, I talked with Jay, a fellow American missionary, from Water for Life, and he just heard that the Peten is closing its border. Traveling at this time may place him in a precarious situation. He could be stuck on the road, taken to jail, or quarantined in a hospital in Guatemala City.

A river may run wild after a storm, with water crashing on the rocks and the shore, producing fear and havoc. Satan, who is a liar, will raise his ugly head in the same way, creating a storm of fear in our mind. Today the wife of a reportedly infected man in the Rio Dulce threw herself off the Rio Dulce bridge. She died, leaving her children behind. Some days are just plain hard. To top it off, Blanca, our nanny, has tears in her eyes today. She is separated from her daughter and explained that her family will not allow her to return home. They are afraid she may become infected with the virus if she goes home. Blanca stayed at Casa Agua Azul for more than a month before her family came to their senses.

When you are in the rapids and jagged rocks are in view, what is dear to your heart will be revealed. I feel the hardest part of this virus is separated families. I am reminded of God and how sin affects our relationship and separates us from Him. Just look at Adam and Eve in the garden. After they ate from the forbidden tree, they hid from God. If you think God was not sad, think again. He has made a way home for his children through his son, Jesus, who suffered greatly. Imagine how that felt to God—to send His only begotten son to be a sacrifice for our sins so we could be reunited. Joy and pain are often mixed. If you think God does not have feelings, then why do we if we are made in the image of God?

Breathe deep as the river flows just around the bend. New hope appears when you least expect it. Peace suddenly comes into your path as the river calms, and so it is a beacon of spiritual light! Casa Agua Azul today is a dream realized!

Casa Agua Azul is God's house filled with love for the children. Guatemala cares for their babies differently than in America—or, at least, in the neighborhood I grew up in. Guatemalans literally hang them up in slings for naptime. I was in a small village hut with my husband when, with much surprise to our eyes, a baby was hung up in the corner of the room like a coat on a rack. The tiny baby was just peering out at us, looking as wide-eyed as a little owl. Naptime for little ones is to be bundled up then strung up to the ceiling or snugly tied and secured into a mini hammock. After a while, this looks normal and is no longer a surprise to the eye.

Rivers twist and turn just as life does. With every twist and turn, there is a lesson to be learned. An adolescent child from the streets with an attitude as tall as the La Ceiba tree I saw on arrival to Casa Agua Azul wore a constant scowl on his face. Today my heart melted watching him tenderly lift up a one-year-old from waking.

A TRAIL OF THE HOLY SPIRIT

He then sets him gently down, placing shoes on the little one's feet, and then they both walk off together. This is what can happen when false pride and deep hurts become cleansed by the love of Christ. It is this love which overcomes any hurt, any harm if you let it in.

The river is the river of life. As the river of life flows, the children are healing because the children are learning to love. They desire love, which they receive here, and they have the opportunity to give love too. Transformation of the heart is taking place; it's not without its troubles and sibling rivalry, but it is happening. Our goal is to not only put a roof over their heads but also a roof over their hearts.

Life teaches many lessons. I am watching tenderness germinate and grow as one of our babies starts to cry. The smaller children will come to comfort. They have a strong, precious love bubbling outward, seen in action. Their hearts are tender toward one another. Our first children, who have been with us for more than a year, are growing into wonderful little people. They are curious and filled with life. During the virus lockdown, the children and I left the confines of the property to break the monotony. We climbed around the fence and tramped through some thick leaves, walking past the fish farm boats into an adventure. It feels so good to walk and be free. The trail is overshadowed by tall trees on the lakefront. Exploring nature brings peace to my heart. Finding the perfect place, we all jumped in the lake and screamed as the seaweed touched our legs. Life happens, and to our surprise, the neighbor's cows decided to walk around the fence, coming closer to us. The children ran and screamed louder the closer they came. Laughter is good medicine, filling our hearts with joy.

Don't fight the river, for it is a ride. Jesus calls us out beyond the waves, and he will make us brave. The deeper we go, the stronger we shall be. How brave do you care to be?

> There is no fear in love, because perfect love casts out fear. (1 John 4:18)

As you surrender your life, you will receive your life from God. It is the flow of the river. Jesus is calling you beyond the waves as heaven awaits.

The ebb and flow move in perfect harmony. While we are here on earth, God is building us into an army. At the same time, we are his beautiful bride being strengthened. We are not created to be weak people—we have a mighty God. Water reflects and acts as a mirror when we are still. In our weakness, God is strong. Jesus is the Alpha, the Omega, the beginning, and the end. He is the one doing a good work and will bring *it*, which is *you*, into completion.

> Be still and know that I am God. (Psalm 46:10)

God is building a home for the children, and you can be an important part of his work here on earth. God uses people like you to promote healing in the children, through love, as the Holy Spirit moves within our hearts. There is a mighty plan and purpose in all things. We each carry a gift within. To walk with the Lord is to walk in uniqueness. Our lives, in his design, will look different from anything we may think or imagine. The Lord will build and create with vessels surrendered willingly to his purposes. He loves to build and create. At the beach, when the surf is up, it's time to go for a ride. Now is the time to ride the wave of the Holy Spirit and be amazed at what God will do! Jesus is coming—be ready. He wants to build his house with you.

As the rain comes, forming a slippery slope, there will be times to surrender to the emerging mud. In life, often things happen outside of your control. I watch the children as siblings hold close to each other as they play. No matter what has happened to them, many are committed to their parents and desire to be reunited. In a small way, I was relating to the children with the comparison of my current state when the world closed borders and I was separated from my husband. The ache inside my heart is powerless to be reunited until the government gives release to borders, similar to the circumstances which the children face, regarding the judicial decisions.

Love runs strong—even abusive love—but God's plan is unity. The law has removed these children from homes due to various forms of abuse and neglect. Some children have no family visitors, causing the rejection they already feel to intensify when other parents arrive. In some cases, the parental visit causes more pain and anguish in their precious hearts. We are here to love them through this. Some will remain until they come of age while others will be reunited to safe family members with good results. Yet, unfortunately, some will go home; and eventually, the abuse will commence. Sadly, the children will continue to go through the system and have their hearts broken again and again. As imperfect as the system may be, it is the law designed to protect. We have to submit and commit no matter what it takes.

I strongly believe the greatest gift we can give is love. We live in a fallen world with free will. Until sin is abolished, abuse will continue. Jesus came to defeat the consequences of sin, which is death. His death on the cross has given us new life and the ability to forgive. The power of the Gospel is truth on the cross, pure love given to birth new love into man's heart. Love has the power to heal. Our foundation at Casa Agua Azul is love—pure love—only found in Jesus.

Casa Agua Azul reflects on the favorite parts of my childhood. I have always had an attraction and love for the Native Americans, running free to explore nature in the woods along the river, visiting our local waterfall, and family time at Crystal Lake in Connecticut swimming, laughing, and playing. These are my childhood treasures, and I'm blessed that our children are able to have similar experiences. Here in Guatemala, the lake is bigger, the falls are warmer, cascading from an underground hot spring. Our location is on the shore of Lake Izabal in an indigenous village. It couldn't be a more perfect place to share my childhood wonders!

Casa Agua Azul was once just a dream which started from a thought. The specially placed dream, living inside my heart, has been there from before the beginning of time. Just as a pearl takes time to cultivate, so will our dreams prior to being lived. I believe dreams are to be lived because why else would God place a dream within our hearts? They are a desire with a heartbeat often buried deep inside until the right moment. As the hunger increases, faith is conjured up to ride the wave of destiny. The waves of love crash in, calling and beckoning for more. The song of your soul desires to be released. The question is are you willing to plunge in and swim in the depths of the ocean of love or just wade on the shores of the lake? To jump is to risk what is human, to receive what is divine, to ride free and to ride love, experiencing the unknown. Confidence to move forward will come as you enter into the throne room of grace.

Grace gives freedom, and our freedom is in being able to choose. Choice without proper action is a stagnant pool where darkness breeds more darkness. It is the running water of life which is free. Freedom grows in hope and love. This is his spirit, the Spirit of God, which is holy. Love never fails; it guides the way. However, the process of love often brings pain. When we allow pain to stop us, the heights of love will never be reached. To push through to the other side will take perseverance on your part. Do not be afraid. Fight tiredness and brokenness, and you will win much more. The tears which flow from your heart will break through the barriers which attempt to hold you back. Your tears may become your greatest advocate. They will be the running water which brings life. To release your tears is freedom. To hold them back produces a motionless pool doomed to murkiness. Just as a beaver dam holds back the flow, we deceive ourselves by betraying our emotional self. God has given us emotions. Emotional intelligence is the ability to perceive and understand emotions in themselves and others, bringing that skill to benefit all. It is a gift not to betray. Use it with wisdom to align our body and mind to come into agreement with his Word—the word of truth. Your godly dream, your life, is within you. I pray for release of what God has stored up within to come forth and run wildly free.

The wave of your dream demands honesty. To be honest is to be brave. You will move mountains and dispel fear as you look into faces and stand in unknown places. Remember, it is the faith of a mustard seed calling you into the depths. Fear must not have its way, for God did not give you a spirit of fear but one of love, power, and a sound mind (2 Timothy 1:7). Every word of your mouth, when chosen according to his Word, spoken in love, is your freedom to ride into the unknown.

Confidence is not yours; it is his, for your confidence is in him and his Word, which is truth. Your choice is to believe in the one God has sent, Jesus, to give you victory. Betrayed trust of the past will stare you down, attempting once again to halt you with false accusations. Question yourself—what have you been trusting in? There is one worthy of trust who will never leave you or forsake you. You may not understand because human reasoning is not capable of divine reasoning. God sees the end from the beginning, but he still gives us wisdom as we ask for it and need it, and he gives us love. Love is greater than understanding, and perfect love casts out fear. Your empowerment, once again, is not your own. Take a look at love; the depths of love are beyond words. Love is often felt, but at the same time, it is often hidden. The greatest love was expressed at the cross by Jesus of Nazareth. The depth of his love is beyond words, human reason, or understanding. His love is freely given to a blind, dark world. God has asked us to believe in the one who was sent. It is in this place that you are able to rest in trust which will never leave you. Confidence is in Jesus Christ and in him alone. Jesus defeated darkness and all the lies of darkness. To ride the wave of the Spirit is to hold close to Jesus. He is magnificent, willing to take you to new heights and depths for one reason—he loves you, and his love is pure.

Don't fight the river—you will never win. Find the ever-present love of God and ride the rapids. I found myself fighting, wanting to be with my husband during the onslaught of the pandemic. With the world going crazy, I craved connection; but the electricity and, subsequently, the Internet at Casa Agua Azul started going out at 4:00 a.m. I felt threatened. However, one morning I found myself renewed; something had changed inside of me. By accepting my disconnection and the unknown, I became aware of and listened more carefully to the early morning sounds as the village started to stir. The sound was a circular chain reaction of dogs barking from one end of the village to the other, with roosters chiming in. Dogs barked from one end of the village, circling around to the other in a chain reaction, as the roosters and the village began to stir. Loud praise from the churches filled the air and never seemed to stop. Peace had settled over the village and over my heart. I got up and looked over the grounds, watching the children at play. Their love for each other was apparent, revealing God's hand and heart at work. Suddenly, I realized I was exactly where God wanted me. The pondering and wondering of my mind ceased as I placed myself and my comfort aside. Only then was I able to ask God, "What can I do for others.?" I felt grateful and fulfilled by this heart transformation.

Jerry and I drove into town for supplies on the third day of the first Corona curfew in Guatemala. The normal bustle of the Rio Dulce had slowed way down. Many shops were closing, but some still remained open. By 1:30 p.m., a group of people on the street started pressuring the police to close all the shops, which did not make sense to me. I asked myself, *Why are they on the street if they want others off the street?* I call it "Corona brain." By the time we left at 2:30 p.m., supplies in hand, Rio Dulce had become a ghost town.

The road from town to home is a very bumpy ride; it is stripped of its pavement and rutted with large potholes due to the truck traffic carrying dirt from the local nickel mines. On one particular section, you need to drive really slowly, or your car will rattle to pieces. This is where I like to pray, and it has become my favorite part of the road. Jerry and I started praying on the way home. Earlier, during our conversation on the way to town, we discovered we were both feeling this weight to the point of exhaustion. It was so intense that for two days, we both had carried it in silence. I thought it was my blood sugar and my need to exercise. Jerry had had a long drive to bring Gaby close to Guatemala City, so we both put it off until now.

Putting two and two together, it became very clear that the oppression revealed did not belong to us. As I said before, spiritual warfare is real and will disguise itself, hoping not to be discovered. Prayer is our weapon to take authority against the looming darkness. We had a great concern with one of our boys and prayed specifically. The children have been victims of sin played out in horrific acts. We provide food and shelter, but if we don't take care of their spirit, we have failed. The spiritual well-being of each child is their future. Someone has to stand in the gap and fight for them while leading them in a new way. Through prayer, we were expecting peace as we pulled into the gates of Casa Agua Azul.

A TRAIL OF THE HOLY SPIRIT

That afternoon was just that—spending time with the children playing in the lake. Before sunset, I took a walk with my two appointed bodyguards. Jerry likes to send the older boys with me—a precautionary protection! I love walking along the shore of the lake to refresh my spirit and to speak life into them. We passed our neighbor's house, being welcomed as if we are family. One sweet dog likes to greet us every time we pass with a wag of a tail and what looks like a smile on his face. Turkeys chuckle and geese squawk; I am not a farm girl by any means, but there is something special here. Everything appears so alive and real. I see a richness in life despite the poverty around me. There is a huge economic difference compared to the United States, but there is a quality within these people that is special. Their ways are so different from mine. I don't understand them, and they don't understand me. I have not been rejected; I am accepted just as I am. The spirit exists beyond language, and love never fails.

One of my big little guys carries his machete and takes pride in being commissioned to lead the way. I strangely feel at home in my discomfort. I stand out, so different, with the continued wonder of *Is there a reason I am here?*

Carrying the machete home, I remember a plastic sword on my bed when I went into the jungle with nine women and saw this ministry being born. God has sent me here for his purpose—"to defend the cause of the weak and the fatherless; to uphold the cause of the poor" (Psalm 82).

When the river is blocked, time will tell you why. Our adventures in life present themselves from the many choices we make. Some are good and others not so good while some are the choices of others; life will happen with much of it out of our control. Patience is learned if you desire peace, and all situations have teachings of importance. We are able to find joy and purpose in the journey.

My journey on the river has taken twists and turns with many blockages. I have traveled through the darkness of caves, survived the rapids, and crashed down many waterfalls. I have fought, and I have surrendered. The sun has shone, and in the darkness there has been rain. I have ridden the height of the wave and wallowed in the depth of despair. Water comes in many forms: hot, cold, frozen, and vapor. It may be clear, cloudy, salty, fresh, or full of debris. The movement varies from still, fast, slow, and everything in between, teaching us that life is full and forever changing.

I finally quit fighting the river and said yes to what was ahead. All I can say is how great is our God, who saved a wretch like me. I once was lost, but now I see. It is the mercy, the grace of God walked out in faith, relying on the true, hidden crown of Christ on the cross. The crown of thorns carries the weight of the world and has all authority here on earth as it is in heaven. To him be all glory, for he is worthy of all our praise. It is the power of his Holy Spirit rising up for justice; truly God is good all the time. He takes what the devil means for harm and turns it for good. Not one minute of your life is wasted when you look to the King of kings. He redeems from death and destruction, giving life to the full. You are a jewel in his crown! All you need to do is believe.

Oh, how God loves faith. I testify to this. He is my testimony—look what Christ has done. He who started a good work in me will bring it to completion, and he will do the same for you. There is a dream in your heart, created for you, that is meant to be lived. Look in your heart; what do you see? What do you feel? What do you dream? Do not be afraid; God says be strong and courageous, for God did not give us a spirit of fear. This is the truth. Grab onto the river of life. It is here, it is flowing, and it is free. Casa Agua Azul, once a vision and a dream, is living water, a reality today, to bless the many children in need.

A TRAIL OF THE HOLY SPIRIT

Momma Blanca with babies

10

The Journey Isn't Over

From a world of lockdown to flooding and a field of dreams, adventure never ceases. My time in Guatemala is a never-ceasing amazement of what will happen next. As I look ahead, personal experience creates growth and gives insight for the development of Casa Agua Azul. We are all grateful that baby Gail is now healthy. No more crying nights. The doctors have diagnosed her well. As I carry her about in the American baby backpack, the nannies laugh as I held her as my own. She is tiny. She is precious. She is a fighter for life. Gaby, now back in the city, continues to send updates from the US Embassy, which is coordinating with commercial carriers to facilitate flights home to the US. World leaders are working together to bring people home. President Trump is interceding on our behalf with President Giammattei for flights to come into Guatemala City, and they are in agreement. Jerry's brother is traveling through Mexico and will be escorted from the border to the airport to fly into the US. God is so present! This virus is attacking the spirit of man; for many, fear and anxiety are taking root; but for others, the strength and power of love is growing across the world. Hope for mankind is emerging; love is coming forth.

My heart is torn between the children and my husband. I have not been away this long under normal circumstances, but during what has become a world crisis, it is nice to be with the man you gave your heart to, the one who supports you with his love, trust, and compassion, which grows stronger every day. Our family is what is dear to us.

One night, my mother's heart for my son went into overload as he was also in the middle of a journey. As any good mother would do, I texted, "Trevor, this virus is bad. The best way to stop it is to stay away from others. God gives you wisdom to walk in faith."

He answered, "I'm not around too many people" with a picture of his motor bike in the desert. I had to laugh—he was just fine! My mom, at ninety-two, was tucked away on a farm of one hundred acres in Connecticut, happy as a clam. Corona brain will get you every once in a while if you are not careful. Isn't it great to love although it may cause one to hit the panic button on occasion!

Of course, the Internet is out, so trying to buy a ticket turns into World War III. I pause and remember that missions take a network of people. Honestly, if it weren't for my husband and Gaby, I would be clueless. We all have our gifts. Sadly, I have to return to America even though I am not quite ready to leave here. March 31, in my mind, would be the perfect departure date. From reading the embassy updates, the thought of "an indefinite period of time abroad "is a motivator. As much as I love it here, I love my husband too! There is a direct flight March 29 into Miami. Suddenly the story of the man on the roof during a flood comes to mind. God told him he had sent him a boat and a plane and more. So God is sending me an airplane! It is not good to look a gift horse in the mouth. Faith is not a license to be stupid because I want something my way. I am not so certain it's a good time to be leisure in purchasing a ticket—flights are limited! I have hesitated on tickets before, which I always regretted. With Gaby's help, I was able to get a ticket. I have three more days here with the children before setting out to Guatemala City.

There are many who need our prayers right now, with family members in the hospital and those who have lost loved ones. People are out of work, and the economy is taking a dive. A missionary friend reports from Honduras that all stores are closed—there is no way for the people to get food. Hearing that made me grateful for all I have here in the house. Life is a precious gift; it is one that cannot be bought. Value it, and at the same time, keep compassion for others, for you are not walking in their shoes. If you are blessed, bless another because we will always have the poor with us. There will always be someone in need; that person may be you one day. God says to do unto others as you would have others do unto you.

The new morning is quiet. Bugs, birds, and the music of nature is present even if all else is quiet. No singing from the church today. Every day is new and different. A knock on the gate brings Delcia in for work. Eventually, the silence is broken; Ludwing is cutting wood with the saw while children's voices are heard. All appears to be normal. Then a jeep drives through the village. A voice over the speakers is giving information, a service provided by the municipality of El Estor. They are going out into the many small villages, giving updates on the virus. This morning they are announcing in Spanish that El Estor, which is our neighboring town, is clean, no cases, but the entrance to town is closed. Do you remember "Hotel California"? No one in or out. I feel like I am in a movie again. I guess I'd better play my part as the American.

I only have a short amount of time left with the children. Soon I will travel to Guatemala City to spend the night with Gaby before boarding a flight. My phone finally rings, and it's my friend Marina on WhatsApp. I am so excited! It is a refreshing moment and spirit building. I get to talk to someone else who understands English! We talk about our recent personal experiences. I love Marina saying, "It is so great to be joyful at this time and for you to be able to spend time with the children and do God's work, to cast out demons and to keep going on, and to write because it's his story!" I need to remind myself what we believe becomes our life; there is more than one world operating out there. It is good to cheer each other on.

My last day with the children started early. There is no sleep after 8:30 a.m. Ludwing is cutting with the saw again. It's the sound of normal! The children fasted this morning and prayed for my safe travel back home to Papa Ted. All twenty-three of us, the children, and nannies, loaded up into two vehicles and headed out on a family outing to a remote river. Leaving our village, we discovered a roadblock. A gate is up at the entrance, with a pole coming down across the road, not allowing people to come or go without being checked.

A TRAIL OF THE HOLY SPIRIT

We are checking out. I am hoping they let *Gringa* back in for the night! Turning onto the main road, we exit near the banana farm to go along the riverbank then cross the river to find a nice shaded area. The nannies are concerned about the babies, which alters our course; it's important to keep our nannies happy! Remember, remain flexible as the plan is always changing. We went back to the main road and got off at another dirt road. As we passed through a remote village, the babies were being rocked to sleep by the rough and raw terrain. It changed to high grass, and a precarious wood bridge was ahead. Then we passed through the bush as if we were on an African safari.

I hope we don't get lost. I am thinking, *How did I get here, driving a bunch of Guatemalans around someplace in the wilderness* as Mama Blanca laughs and says, "It's okay, Mama Gail!" Being from the Florida Keys, I see water ahead, which always feels like home to me. We have arrived a bit further down the river than we planned. It is very flat and desert-looking on one side. A dry rock bed is running with the river while on the other side, it is mountainous, green, and steep. The river is shallow with a few deep pockets where the current is flowing. The rocks in the river are spectacular. I have a few for my suitcase. It's a habit of mine. I just really love rocks. It's hard to pass up a good rock. White, red, and gold are highlighted by the sun's rays through the clear water. The children are exploring, squealing with excitement, jumping in, and floating down the mini rapids. As I watch our Casa Agua Azul family, I see how all interact with each other; they flow in such unity. It is certain the children are being well cared for. I am impressed with their ability to work as a unit, loving each other well. It was a beautiful day, ending my time, for now with the children.

The next morning, with Jerry driving, our trip to Guatemala City is uneventful. It's hard to get up early to leave at 6:00 a.m.; I am a night person. Trucks are on the road, and the city is active; but at 4:00 p.m., everything shuts down. We arrived at the city at a good time, around 1:00 p.m. You do not want to be out after curfew. They take the curfew seriously, and you will end up in jail if you are out. My throat was starting to feel scratchy, so I was feeling nervous about my flight in the morning. I started thinking, *What if they take me away to the hospital, believing I have the virus?*

My continued favorite place to stay in the city is at Faithful Steps mission house! Currently Gaby, along with her siblings and nieces, continue to open their family home to us and our mission teams—another home away from home. I pray all night for healing in my throat. In the morning, I feel great except when I go to speak, my voice is super deep! Hopefully the people at the airport will not notice. If they become suspicious of you, they may take you to quarantine. I believe that is why they only have thirty-two cases in the country at this time.

I am elated to see my husband today in Miami. It's been quite the journey. I love my Guatemalan friends, and I look forward to returning as soon as the borders are open again. The streets are empty today because it is Sunday. Arriving at the airport was an "oh my goodness!" moment and a realization that maybe we should have left earlier. About one thousand people were outside, waiting. They were all dressed in similar attire and had a sense of unity. I do not understand why so many Canadian flags were everywhere as the next flight out was going to Wyoming. There was no one representing the United States or Eastern Airlines!

Walking over to the entrance to find out where to go, I was very grateful Jerry was by my side. My Spanish still needs some work! The officials were taking temperatures and said they knew nothing of this flight to Miami. Next to me are a few others with tickets to Miami, five of us in total, my new *amigos*. We became very united before we left the airport, all in different directions. I asked Gaby and Ted to call the airlines. Without notice, they had canceled the flight! The airline is short-staffed and overloaded. Our flight was rescheduled for the next day at 1:00 p.m. What is one to do but remember to be flexible and say, "Okay, thank you very much!"

I was grateful to have my friends in the city. Returning to the house, I made brownies with the young girls. Gaby and Debora taught me how to make pineapple tea. Then we all went up to the rooftop to hang out, praising, singing, and dancing. Jerry started the long drive back to the Rio Dulce, and with the curfew, he will not be able to make it all the way back. Not knowing the language is difficult at a time like this. God's hand was upon me. At that moment,

A TRAIL OF THE HOLY SPIRIT

I had a certain level of comfort seeing the airport scene and meeting my flight mates Marie, Daniel, and Lester. Feelings are subject to change. I have learned in my travels to rely on the Holy Spirit. He has always sent someone to guide me along the way. A cell phone is also a great comfort!

Departing Guatemala is very emotional. Gaby walked me to the entrance of the airport. After hugging her, I went inside, with tears just welling up in my eyes. The intensity of love I was experiencing was overwhelming my heart. Making my way through security and immigration, the waves of love continued to intensify. God's love for the world is so magnificent. When I looked out the airport window, I saw the plane's passengers disembarking. There was an elderly man in a wheelchair, and I imagined his family must be so grateful to have their loved one home.

Guatemalans are coming home. The airport attendant walked up to me and asked, "France?" Each country is coming for their people to bring them home. I see the love and kindness people have for each other. It is interesting to watch how important it is for countries to get their people home. I think of a snake recoiling and what is coming next to the world.

As I waited in silence for my plane to board, my mind was all over the place. People stood far apart from each other, and that did not change once we were on the plane. It was as if we were all in our own cocoon. At last, I arrived at Miami International Airport; just as the flight was very sparse, Miami's airport was also empty. Walking the halls through customs and immigration, no one said a word. It is utter silence. My husband pulls up to the empty curb, and I wonder, *Was I just in a dream?*

God's timing is perfect. One day, after being back in the States, the police and the health department came to Casa Agua Azul. They searched the property, looking for the American! As they asked many questions, Jerry was assuring them that I am well, but not there: "She has gone back to the States." But she will be back!

Jesus makes us brave for the days to come; life is a series of letting go and embracing. My eyes are filled with tears; it is the incredible power of love, echoing God's overwhelming love.

Our adventures in life present themselves from the many choices we make—some good and others not so good—but all have teachings of importance. In this way, we are able to find joy and purpose in our journey.

Days, weeks, and months pass. There are many opinions and attitudes with the various reports of what is best, with the pandemic making the news and becoming old news. Our US presidential election and threatening hurricanes steal attention from the pandemic but only for the moment.

After waiting out many hurricanes that rose out of the ocean eight months into the Coronavirus, Ted and I were finally making preparations to sail back to Guatemala. Our original plan was to sail in August, but the borders did not open until September 2020; then hurricanes became very active. For months, I was waking up with constant dreams of muddy water filled with debris. I was disturbed and asked God to interpret the dreams. I was especially wondering if there was something in my own life that was out of order. As we packed our vessel and prepared for departure, many unknowns ahead would soon be revealed.

As the eye of hurricane Eta passed over our home in the Florida Keys with minimal damage, I still did not connect with my dreams. Central America was in a dire situation with rain continuing to fall for weeks on end. Eta had left a path of destruction by flooding and destroying homes and lives. If that was not enough, Hurricane Iota was blazing the same trail. We set sail just prior to Iota with a cold front barreling down the coast of Florida. The winds were in our favor, and our mission vessel was heavily loaded with supplies.

The heavy seas merged with high winds as the cold front met the outer rings of Iota. Needless to say, the water was stirred up and raging. We sailed five days of a "Maytag special," being tossed around in the ocean with seas pounding on our hulls. To our experienced crew of world-class racing sailors, it was a good day and ride. The blessing of our crossing was that of following seas, which makes all the difference in the world. Even so, for the novice sailor, the rocking and rolling was intense and disorientating.

A TRAIL OF THE HOLY SPIRIT

In life we are powerless over many things, yet in these moments, choices still confront us. As we arrived at the Rio Dulce of Guatemala, the flooding was increasing. As I looked at the muddy water filled with debris, I started to understand my dream, knowing it was no accident we were here.

The many medical supplies, blankets, clothing, and baby supplies packed onboard were right on time. We spent the next few weeks unloading, going out to Casa Agua Azul, and joining the relief efforts of the community. Then it was time for my husband, Ted, to journey back to the states. Our friends from Boatique Marina picked him up in their boat to catch an early morning flight with missionary pilot Jason. I was remaining behind for another week before joining Ted and our family in Texas.

During this time, Jerry and Gris had invited me to join them to travel to a family wedding, and they seemed very excited for me to partake in this adventure. So I went for a ride called the Great Adventure with Gris! After traveling five or six hours in the car, a sign for Mexico was on the horizon. I was wondering where exactly we were going. As we passed the sign, we went in a different direction. The mountains had turned to hills and now into flat farmlands. We continued driving. Gris laughed and asked me how I liked my adventure. She has a good sense of humor. The change in scenery was relaxing. The small towns and villages were now total wilderness, looking like Africa. If a hippo appeared, it would look totally natural.

Eventually, we came to an area of commerce. Stopping in the bustling town, we purchased our supplies for the weekend ahead. We were close to our destination but still not there. I was imagining in my mind we were going to a large ranch to attend a family wedding, so when we turned off the main road to a dirt road, it fit with the image in my mind. The road was dusty, flat, straight, and well-maintained. A small *tuk-tuk* passed us in the opposite direction, a strange place for this three-wheeled vehicle that is used to transport people. A while later, we slowed down as a herd of sheep crossed our path. The land was fenced off into large parcels where cattle, goats, and sheep grazed. Many new young ones were seen in the herds. Forty minutes later, we passed a *tienda*, which is a very small store. This place is well known as a spot where you can pick up a cell signal, but not today, tomorrow, or the next day.

The writing of my experiences and thoughts is coming to a close. I am sitting next to a tractor—the least likely place I would imagine finding myself—with the sounds of geese and other noises foreign to my ears. In life, we may often wonder why we are here or there. We also may not know the answer, but it is faith that allows you to know wherever you are, there is a higher purpose. One day, as you ponder, you will see why.

It was dark when we arrived at El Mango, a small Guatemalan village not far from the Mexican border, surrounded by an expanse of uninhabited jungle. The village formed from people who once came to hide during the American Civil War and also those fleeing from Mexico. Today it has a population of nearly six hundred.

We were greeted with smiles and invited into the preparation for the festival. I was introduced to the many family members, and when they realized I did not speak Spanish, we had many laughs along with them sharing what they knew of the English language. I was wondering how I was going to fit in and communicate. My hope was as I observed my surroundings, I would intuitively know what to do next. I was feeling immensely awkward.

People were enjoying fresh beef and tortillas with tomato sauce and beans, just like any other family gathering, laughing and loving each other. When we walked next door, I saw the source of the beef—freshly slaughtered and being butchered. The sight to a vegetarian was not one of delight but of interest. When the ax penetrated the bone to separate the meat, I gladly volunteered to help snap the one hundred pounds of green beans. There were also five hundred pounds of potatoes to be peeled! I watched a girl carry a large sack on her head, and I wanted to try it. It is an art, one which I was not able to have success in. I asked Gris if she was able to do this. I was amazed as she placed the large heavy sack on her head and danced.

Life is like a river containing many twists and turns. I snapped beans with the ladies and children throughout the night. I found myself being showered with green bean ends by the young boys. My survival mechanism was teaching English words for common items;

in this way, I made new friends and had fun. As I think of the river of life, my dreams of the night showed the force of a wave and then the soft white foam that goes ashore, carrying that which is upon it.

I am sitting here in this land where men wear guns strapped to their hips and plug in their cell phones. The gun I see a use for, but if you stay out here, a cell phone and your credit card will be of no use. There is no way I am able to call my husband from here; I miss being with him. I then realize if I did not come here, I would not see into the life and family of those who live in this land. The children we care for at Casa Agua Azul will one day be removed from the protective walls of the home. What and how we teach them will enable them to survive or thrive in their own river of life.

I felt that I was being carried by the white foam of the wave in my prior night's dream. The wedding was fun and beautiful. After helping serve the large vats of meat which simmered over a wood fire all night long, I found my dance card full to music I had never heard before.

In the morning, a big surprise awaited. I was not able to walk. My tendons were strained and screaming. Walking was now hobbling with a wrenching grin, but our adventure was ongoing and running in high gear. Why stop now—the damage is done. Let's get rolling! We drove out even deeper into the jungle hills to the ranch. This is where I rode a horse and helped herd the cattle into new fields. This was absolutely the most fun and highlight of the trip, but there was more! Next was a motorcycle ride. We rode deep through a tikka forest; the beauty stole my heart. Eventually, we stopped at Gris's land, and there we prayed into a field of dreams. We know that "prayer availeth much."

The property, in past years, did not have a pond on it. Currently there is a pond which breeds shrimp, where Gris graciously allows the poor of the community to come and find food. In my world, shrimp live in the ocean, but I have learned to just go with the flow here. Many things make no sense at all to me, so I have quit trying to make sense. After all, I am on an adventure! Eventually, we worked our way back to town. By 8:00 p.m., we were on the road, headed back to the river with half a cup of coffee. Driving through the night, we arrived at Casa Agua Azul at 4:00 a.m. What an adventure!

With a day of rest, we are on the move again. Part of our responsibility for the children, mandated by the government, is to work with the families. Three of our children—two girls and one boy—came from the port town of Livingston. They are from a family of seven dearly loved children. Sadly, their father passed away, placing them in a desperate situation. Their mother remarried into what became an abusive relationship, eventually separating. The children miss their home and their mom. At night, the young boy cries for his mom. Jerry, Hany, our social worker, and I traveled to Livingston with the oldest of the three in our care in hopes of visiting with the mom and bringing comfort to their hearts. We were able to meet with her older sister and her grandmother. However, her mom has fallen into alcohol abuse and was not to be found. It was a sad ride home.

The children come from poverty in many forms. I would like to share with you a home I personally witnessed. Built over a stream was a small cute-looking house surrounded by hanging laundry, with the sweetest kitten hanging out in the outdoor kitchen. The kitchen was not much more than a couple of pieces of metal on a wooden structure with wood for the fire and a few buckets for washing. The inside of the house caught my attention, and I pondered my surroundings. The window area had plastic bags and old tattered sheets instead of windows. One tiny lone refrigerator with a streak of rust stood next to one wall. Our host set out two white plastic chairs while she sat on a laundry basket between a bucket and a small welding machine next to an unidentifiable metal object in the corner. Next, I looked around to see cardboard in the rafters near the worn faded hammock. On the far side of the L-shaped room, which is the entire home, was a wooden box, about three feet by five feet, with clothes stored in it. Other than these items, there were a few pieces of clothing strewn about the rafters. The floor had open crevices, and the door to the front porch was a sheet with a chicken sitting on the other side. We did not see a bathroom. I was challenged to think deeper because Jerry, our director, said that this house is a million times better than the house of one of our other boys.

My heart is heavy in my chest, feeling the deep bonds of love running between mother, father, and child. A child's longing for their parents' love never ceases. We will never take their place. What is best for the child is in God's hand. Casa Agua Azul is here to do our part.

There is a cost to changing lives, but there is a greater cost not to.

And so it is with the wind of the Spirit.

A jungle home

Our beautiful nannies

The beginning

A TRAIL OF THE HOLY SPIRIT

Joy complete

Casa Agua Azul Today

GAIL GORDON

> As you journey and grow with the Holy Spirit,
> may you know Him in a greater
> capacity and be His hands and feet.
> For nothing will be impossible with God.
> Luke 1:37

Gabriella a Voyage of Faith

About the Author

Gail Gordon's home base is in the Florida Keys. Her greatest joy in life has been to raise her son, Trevor, with her husband, Ted. Having raised her son, she now travels extensively between the United States, Guatemala, and the Bahamas.

God's creation brings life to her soul. She has a great love for sailing especially on the ocean with its many moods. This zeal was birthed in her soul as she sailed with her family in and through the South Pacific on a journey of faith.

With a heart for adventure, she invites others to journey with her as she leads mission teams onboard her sailboat, *Viento Azul* (worship-sailing.com https://www.sailblogs.com/member/worship-sailing/).

After raising her son, Trevor, she founded Casa Agua Azul, a children's home in Guatemala in the Rio Dulce region, and is the director of Blue Water Surrender, a Florida 501 (c) 3 (bluewatersurrender.org).

People matter. She is passionate for others to walk in freedom and know they are a child of God. Her deep compassion for the oppressed has led her to study Christian healing with Global Awakening.

Printed in the USA
CPSIA information can be obtained
at www.ICGtesting.com
LVHW091323221223
767218LV00066B/1839